The World Into Which Jesus Came

by Sylvia Root Tester
illustrated by Mina Gow McLean

Distributed by Standard Publishing,
Cincinnati, Ohio 45231.

THE CHILD'S WORLD

ELGIN, ILLINOIS 60120

Edited by: The Child's World Editorial Staff
Consultant: Thomas D. Thurman, A.B., M.A., M.S.

Distributed by Standard Publishing, 8121 Hamilton Avenue,
Cincinnati, Ohio 45231.

Library of Congress Cataloging in Publication Data

Tester, Sylvia Root, 1939-
   The world into which Jesus came.

   Includes index.
   Summary: Briefly outlines the history of the Jewish
people and describes life in Judea and Palestine during
the time of Jesus, including Jewish laws and customs,
religious and political groups, and the homes, food,
clothing, and occupations of the people.
   1. Jews — Civilization — Juvenile literature.
2. Palestine — Civilization — Juvenile literature.
3. Jesus Christ — Childhood — Juvenile literature.
[1. Jews — Civilization. 2. Palestine — Civilization]
I. McLean, Mina Gow, ill. II. Title.
DS112.T47 1982   956.94'004924   82-9430
ISBN 0-89565-232-3   AACR2

1 2 3 4 5 6 7 8 9 10 11 12 R 89 88 87 86 85 84 83 82

Contents

1394

Before Jesus Came

Jesus was born in a little town called Bethlehem in an area of the world we now call Israel. At the time of Jesus' birth, the area was called Judea. It was the home of the Jewish people. Jesus was born a Jew.

What was the world like at the time Jesus was born? What was Judea like? What were the homes like? the schools? the food? the clothes? the religions? the jobs?

This book will attempt to answer these questions. But first it will present a little background of the Jewish people.

The Jewish people knew their history. They could trace their roots back thousands of years, to Abram (Abraham), who left his homeland in obedience to God.

The Jews knew that God chose Moses to lead the people out of Egypt to the promised land. They knew of their judges and priests, their great king, David, and their prophets.

They also knew that God had promised them a Savior, a Messiah. The promise had been given to Abraham. "In you," God told Abraham, "all the families of the world will be blessed."

Moses knew of God's promise of a Messiah. So did David. And the prophets said many things about this Savior. "He'll be a king in David's line," they said. "A man acquainted with sorrows."

"From Bethlehem," Micah said, "will come the ruler of Israel."

At the time of Jesus' birth, many Jews were ready for Him to come.

Here are some pictures showing the beginning of the world and the history of God's people from the time of Adam and Eve up until the time of Jesus.

© 1962 Standard Publishing

In the beginning, God created the world. He created the heavens above, the earth below. He created the sea, the land, the plants, the animals. Then He created people.

By Noah's time, there were many people. And most of them were evil. So God sent a flood to destroy the earth. Only Noah and his family, and some animals, were saved.

4

Abraham   Isaac   Jacob

Abraham was the father of the Jewish people. He left Ur of the Chaldees to go to a land God promised him. God said Abraham's people would be a great people.

Two of Abraham's sons were Ishmael and Isaac. Jews are descendants of Isaac. Isaac, like Abraham, was faithful to God and kept God's commandments.

Jacob and Esau were Isaac's sons. Although Esau was the older, Isaac's special blessing went to Jacob. God's promise of a Savior was continued through Jacob.

Jacob had many sons. One of them, Joseph, was sold as a slave into Egypt. In Egypt, Joseph became very important. Later, Joseph brought his family to Egypt.

The Israelites stayed in Egypt many years. But after Joseph died, the Egyptians made the Israelites slaves. Then God freed the Israelites, and Moses led them out of Egypt. God parted the sea for them, and they walked safely to the other side. For 40 years, the Israelites wandered in the wilderness. Finally, they came to Canaan, their promised land.

Deborah   Gideon   Samson

Joshua led the Israelites into the promised land. The first town they attacked was Jericho. God made the walls of Jericho fall. The Israelites conquered much of Canaan.

Judges guided Israel for many years. Deborah was one of the judges. She was also a prophetess. Gideon was another judge. He led the people wisely. Samson was still another judge. He was strong, but not very wise. There were a number of judges. Some of the others were named Othniel, Ehud, Shamgar, Tola, Jair, Jephthah, Ibzan, Elon, and Abdon.

A Gentile (non-Jewish) woman is important in Jewish history. Her name was Ruth. Ruth came to Israel with Naomi. Ruth was the great-grandmother of King David.

Samuel is very important in Jewish history. His mother brought him to the tabernacle (God's house) when he was a child. Samuel grew up there, serving the Lord.

The first king of Israel was Saul. In the beginning, Saul was a good king. He followed God's commandments. Later, though, Saul turned away from God.

The next king was David. David was a shepherd when he was young. While guarding his sheep, he killed a lion, and a bear. In battle, David killed the giant, Goliath.

David was a close friend of Jonathan, King Saul's son. After Saul died, David became king. David loved God and tried to obey Him.

David wrote many of the psalms. One of the best known of his psalms begins, "The Lord is my shepherd; I shall not want." Many psalms speak of God's care.

Solomon, David's son, became king after David died. The queen of Sheba traveled thousands of miles to see Solomon's riches and hear him speak wisely. King Solomon built the first temple of God. It was a beautiful building. Solomon brought in huge cedars from Lebanon for the temple. And he used silver and gold to decorate it.

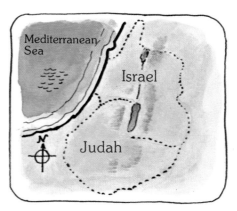

After Solomon died, the people rebelled. Israel became two kingdoms. Rehoboam, ruled Judah. Jeroboam ruled the rest of Israel.

Prophets of God arose in both kingdoms. Elijah and Elisha brought God's messages to kings. Isaiah and Jeremiah told of Jesus' coming.

In 587 B.C., the Babylonians captured Jerusalem and destroyed the temple Solomon had built on Mount Zion. (Israel had been destroyed earlier. Now Judah was captured.) The Babylonians took many Jews back as captives. A psalm tells how the Jews felt: "By the rivers of Babylon, there we sat down, yea, we wept, when we remembered Zion."

One of the Jews in Babylon was Daniel. Daniel refused to pray to a false god. So he was thrown into a den of starving lions. But God closed the lions' mouths.

In 539 B.C., King Cyrus, of Persia, took over the Babylonian empire. Cyrus let many of the captured Jews go back home. Some went back to Jerusalem that same year. Cyrus told them they could rebuild their temple. They began, but didn't get very far. A few years later, more Jews returned. By 515 B.C., the new temple was built.

During the years of captivity, a Persian king made a Jewish maiden, Esther, his queen. Esther saved her people from a plot to kill all of them.

The Persian empire lasted many years. Then, in about 333 B.C., Alexander the Great, a Greek, captured Palestine. The Greeks were powerful for many years.

In 63 B.C., Jerusalem was captured by the Romans. The Romans made "Herod the Great" king of the Jews in 37 B.C. When Jesus was born, Rome was still in charge.

Meet Michael and His Family

(Michael, his family, and his friends, are fictional characters. But the statements about their lives accurately show the way people lived at the time of Jesus' birth. Michael is used throughout this book.)

Michael was a Jewish boy, 12 years old, who lived in Palestine in Jesus' time. His father was a skilled carpenter. Michael's mother was a grand cook and knew how to weave beautiful cloth.

Michael had a sister named Naomi, who was nine years old, and a baby brother named Matthew.

Michael and his family were not rich people. They had a very simple home, typical of the homes in which most of the people lived. The walls were made from clay. Sometimes, there were white patches on the walls. These were from saltpeter, which had worked its way out of the clay.

The windows in Michael's house were small and high, simply holes in the wall.

In Michael's home, the floor was made of dirt, packed hard and smooth. (Some houses had a sunken fireplace in the floor.) At night, Michael would get his sleeping mat and spread it out on the floor. If he needed a blanket, he would use his cloak.

Everyone in the family slept on the floor.

The family members spent much of their time outside because the house was small. They often ate in the courtyard. And they did much of their work either in the courtyard or on the roof.

wineskin

place in wall for storing grain

oil lamp

window—small enough so a thief could not climb through

walls—clay

sleeping mats

large jar for food storage

jar for water

meal tub, or bushel (to store grain in—upside down, it's a table.)

broom

floor—hard-packed dirt (Michael's mother kept the floor swept clean.)

hand mill for grinding flour

Many families built a small room on the roof of the house. Guests slept there. And during the feast of Tabernacles, families often built small booths on the roof.

wall around roof

roof

stairway to roof

Women cooked the bread in round ovens. All cooking was done outside. Grass was used for the fire, since wood was scarce.

Poor people built houses like this one, out of clay. Richer people might have had houses built of limestone or bricks. The bricks were made by mixing clay and straw. Then the bricks were baked in a kiln. Rich people might have had floors of lime and sand, or of brick, and rich people had large homes, with many rooms and lots of fancy furniture.

Meet Michael's Neighbors

Michael lived in the town of Capernaum. His friend, David, lived just down the street. David's father was a merchant. Peter, another friend of Michael, lived on the street, too. Peter's father was a fisherman.

Naomi's friend, Martha, lived next door to Michael and Naomi. Michael and Naomi's mother and Martha's mother often ground grain together. It was easier when two people worked together.

Michael saw many, many people go up and down his street.

Travelers came from many cities and passed through Capernaum. Sometimes Michael walked along with them. Sometimes they told him about faraway countries.

Soldiers in the Roman army often marched by. Michael didn't like the soldiers. None of the Jews liked the soldiers. The Jewish people wanted to rule their own country.

Every evening, women went by on their way to the town's well, and then returned, carrying jars full of water on their heads.

Roman soldiers

Martha's house

Michael's house

woman coming from the well

traveler from Caesarea Philippi

David's house

Peter's house

Mediterranean Sea

Tyre

Achzib

Capernaum

Sea of Galilee

Tiberias

Nazareth

Jordan River

Jericho

Jerusalem

Sometimes, people built their houses right against the city wall. They used the city wall as one wall in the house. From their rooftops they could see the countryside.

Capernaum, where Michael lived, was on the shore of the Sea of Galilee. It was on several main trade routes. A Roman garrison of soldiers was stationed there.

Clothes to Wear

The clothes that Michael wore were very simple. Not only the clothes but the cloth itself was made by his mother. Probably it was made from wool or linen.

First, Michael would put on a shirt. It looked like a nightgown without sleeves. It probably reached down below his knees.

Next, Michael would put on a coat, open down the front. It might be striped. The sleeves would be long, large, and loose. It, too, would reach below Michael's knees.

And it was warm and comfortable.

Michael would add a long strip of cloth called a girdle to this. He'd wrap it around his waist, like a belt. It would keep his coat closed in front. If his father sent him to buy something, Michael would slip the money into his girdle where it would be safe.

Michael could pull up the bottom of the coat and tuck it in his girdle when he wanted to run. Then, he could use the coat as a pocket.

Around home, Michael went

barefooted. If Michael traveled, he usually wore sandals. A sandal had a sole or bottom made of animal skin. Straps of leather kept the sole on Michael's foot.

When the weather was chilly, Michael added a heavy woolen cloak. A cloak looked sort of like a blanket. It was a shawl with arm-holes. At night, he'd use the cloak as a blanket while he slept.

Michael also wore a small hat, a band, a turban, or other head covering.

Michael's father's clothes were much like Michael's. At prayer times, his father also wore two phylacteries. A phylactery was a leather box bound to the forehead or arm with a leather band. Inside was some parchment with Scripture verses on it.

Michael's mother's clothes were similar. Instead of a turban, she wore a long cloth on her head. Sometimes, she would pull the covering over her mouth and nose. But usually, it just covered her head and shoulders. Sometimes she wore coins on her forehead.

Rich men wore the same kinds of clothes, but of course their clothes were much fancier. The weave was much finer and more colors were used. Rich people especially liked the color purple, since purple dye was expensive. A rich man might also wear much jewelry.

In Michael's time, getting new clothes was not easy. First, Michael's mother had to get some wool or flax. From this, she would spin her thread.

With the thread, Michael's mother would weave cloth. She used a loom when weaving. She strung the thread up and down. Then she wove back and forth.

Finally, Michael's mother would cut out and sew together a garment. She had to sew every stitch by hand. Styles were very simple. There were not many seams.

Rich women wore fancy garments and beautiful, imported head coverings. Some of them wore lots and lots of jewelry—rings, bracelets, necklaces, and earrings. The jewelry was all made by hand. Sometimes it was made from gold or silver.

Michael and Naomi are dressed comfortably here — no coats and no sandals. They are out for a walk with their parents and baby brother, Matthew.

Michael's Favorite Foods

Michael was like most children. He liked to eat. His favorite foods were figs and the honey cakes his mother baked for special occasions. But he also liked fish and cheese, goat's milk and mutton (sheep) stew. And he loved the bread his mother made.

Usually, Michael's family ate two main meals every day. But Michael might have a little bread with butter and honey when he got up in the morning. In the middle of the day, Michael might eat bread, cheese, and some grapes. In the evening, he might eat bread, olives, figs, and vegetables. Sometimes there were eggs or fish. Once in a while, Michael's mother would make a delicious stew of sparrow meat or mutton with vegetables. Michael loved to dip his bread in the stew.

Children drank goat's milk. Adults might drink water or a sour wine that was like vinegar.

Have you ever heard of eating grasshoppers? Perhaps Michael did. Many people ate roasted locusts. These were crunchy and salty. People liked them. And sometimes people made locust bread. They would dry the insects, then grind them up into a powder.

They'd mix the powder in with flour, and add a little honey.

Jesus and Food

Jesus' first miracle involved drink. He changed water to wine at a wedding. Read John 2:1-11.

Jesus performed two miracles in which he fed people. In one, He fed over 5,000 from a boy's lunch of five loaves and two fishes. Read Matthew 14:15-21 and Mark 6:35-44. In the other, He fed 4,000 people. Read Mark 8:1-9.

Jesus talked about food in the Sermon on the Mount. Read Matthew 7:9-11.

Jesus spoke often of bread. Read Matthew 4:4 and Matthew 6:11. Jesus said, "I am the bread of life" (John 6:35, NIV*).

Jesus and His disciples ate a last meal together before His death. Read Matthew 26:20-29.

To bake bread, first women ground grain to make flour. They poured grain into the hole in the top stone of the mill. Then they turned the top stone.

*NIV means *New International Version* of the Bible.

Next, a woman made bread dough. She would start with flour. She would add water and leaven. She would knead the dough and let it rise.

When the bread dough was the right size, the woman would shape it into small, round, flat pieces. On special occasions, she might make fancier bread.

Finally, the woman would bake the bread in the oven. The oven shown is one kind of oven. Some women baked over a fireplace or used smaller jar ovens.

15

Plants

Michael would have known about many plants. There were sycamore trees (different from our sycamore trees) and date palm trees and olive trees. Oak trees also grew in the area. They were a special kind of evergreen oak, often more like a bush than a tree. Michael would have known fig trees by sight.

Some bushes grew near Capernaum. And thistles grew everywhere. Thistles may have been the "thorns" in Jesus' parable of the Sower.

Michael certainly knew about wheat and barley. They were important crops in Palestine.

sea daffodils   sunflowers   poppies   iris   crocuses

Israel has hundreds of kinds of wild flowers, and probably did in Bible times, too. There are beautiful irises and crocuses, daisies, poppies, red anemones, and sunflowers. There are sea daffodils named *Pancratium maritimum*. Many people think these white daffodils are the "lilies of the field" Jesus talked about. Others think Jesus meant all the wild flowers in bloom right then. In the rainy season, many wild flowers bloom at once. They can cover whole fields with brilliant color.

Jesus spoke of the mustard seed in a parable. The mustard seed is very tiny. But the plant that grows from it sometimes grows to be twelve feet tall.

The sycamore trees that grow in Palestine live for hundreds of years. They have a fruit that many poor people gather for food. Zacchaeus climbed a sycamore.

One of the worst weeds in Palestine was darnel. Darnel is the "tare" Jesus talked about. When darnel is young, it looks like wheat. Read Matthew 13:24-30.

16

King Solomon brought in giant cedar trees to build his temple and his palace. These trees came from the Lebanon mountains. The Lebanon mountains are north of Palestine. Some of these mountains are 10,000 feet high.

At one time, giant cedar trees covered the hillsides of the Lebanon mountains. But there aren't many cedars left now.

These trees grow to a height of 100 feet. Around their trunks, they are 50 to 65 feet. (Measure that with a tape measure.) The cedars of Lebanon were truly giant trees. Their trunks were straight, and the wood was hard. They were perfect for building beautiful buildings.

People think that the largest cedar tree still living is over 2,000 years old. That means it was a young tree when Jesus lived on the earth.

Animals

Our made-up friend, Michael, would have known about many animals. Perhaps his family kept a sheep for wool or a goat for milk. (Sometimes, a shepherd would take care of the townspeople's sheep in the daytime, bringing the sheep back to town at night.) Michael's parents also might have kept a few chickens so they could have eggs.

And Michael would have known about all the small animals that scampered about, such as mice and hares and coneys (rabbit-sized guinea pigs). He would have seen deer and gazelle and wild goats. He'd have known about partridges, quail, vultures, owls, sparrows, and swallows.

Pigeons and doves were used in sacrifices. Mary and Joseph offered a dove when they took baby Jesus to the temple.

People in Palestine feared wolves, for wolves ran in packs and could be fierce fighters. Often, they attacked sheep. Shepherds sometimes had to fight them off. Foxes were another kind of predator. They caught chickens if they could. And they stole grapes from the vineyard. But they weren't as large or fierce as wolves.

Donkeys, or asses, were common in Palestine. They were used as pack animals, to carry baggage or people. There were also wild donkeys in the area.

The donkey was a work animal. There were other work animals as well. Oxen were used for plowing the fields. Often, two were used together. They were put in a common yoke. Camels carried goods and people. But only the rich owned camels or horses. Horses pulled the Roman commanders' chariots. Some Roman soldiers also rode horses. Even back then, riders on horses carried mail and news from place to place. Some mules were used as riding animals. Sometimes dogs helped shepherds.

Animals that provided food included sheep, goats, and fowls. Gentiles (non-Jews) used hogs for food, although Jewish people would not eat hogs.

Fierce predatory animals (that kill for food) included leopards, cheetahs, lions, bears, hyenas, eagles, hawks. There were also snakes, lizards, and frogs.

Insects were everywhere. Bees made honey. Ants scurried about, busy at their work. Spiders spun their webs wherever they could. Scorpions were to be avoided.

Going Places

If you and I decide to take a trip, we have many choices. We might fly to the place where we're going. Or, we could ride in a car or take a bus or train. We might even ride in a truck or on a motorcycle. Over water, we might take a ship.

If we want to go the hard way, we can ride bicycles, paddle a canoe, sail in a sailboat, or even walk or run. We have many ways of travel from which to choose.

Michael didn't have all these choices. If he had been rich, he could have gone to sea on a large sailing ship. He could have traveled over land on horseback, or in a chariot pulled by horses, or on camelback. But Michael wasn't rich!

It's true that some ordinary people rode mules or donkeys, but Michael's family only had one donkey. They usually used the donkey to carry their belongings while they walked alongside.

In a car, people think nothing of traveling 500 miles in a day. But if people are walking, how far can they go in a day?

A good steady walker can walk about three miles in an hour. Could you walk that fast?

On the Appalachian Trail, which only hikers use, shelters are placed every seven miles. That way, slow hikers can go seven miles in a day. Medium hikers can go 14 miles. Strong, fast hikers can go 21 miles.

If Michael and his family went on a trip, how far do you think they could walk in a day? Remember, someone always had to carry the baby, Matthew. And Michael's sister, Naomi, was only nine.

All these difficulties didn't keep people from traveling, though. Jesus and His disciples walked all over Palestine. So did many other people.

In Bible times, there were no gas or electric or diesel engines. The only kinds of power for water travel were the wind and manpower. The fishermen on the Sea of Galilee used small sailboats. Sometimes, they rowed these boats. On the Mediterranean Sea, large sailing ships traveled from city to city.

20

Buying Things

Instead of buying something, Michael's parents would often barter or trade for it. Michael's mother might trade cloth she had woven for a lamp and some oil.

Sometimes, instead of trading things, people traded work. Michael's father might trade a day's carpentry work for some grain from a farmer or fish from a fisherman.

Michael's family did not have a lot of money. Michael's father received money for his carpentry work, but it was usually spent for food.

The Romans had a system of money that used coins of many kinds. Most of their coins were silver. Some were gold or bronze or copper. Often, the coins had pictures on them.

King Herod the Great had copper coins made. He put palm branches, anchors, grapes, and prows of ships on his coins. His sons ordered the same kinds of pictures on the coins they had made.

Before Jesus was born, Jewish people made their own coins. These coins had Jewish symbols on them. In Jesus' time, leaders of the temple would accept only Jewish coins. Money changers traded people these special coins for their Roman money. Then the temple leaders would accept the people's offerings.

Learning

In Palestine, a family was expected to train every son for a trade. Usually, the first son learned his father's trade. Michael was learning to be a carpenter.

This was not the only kind of training Michael received, though. At home, he was taught to say certain prayers and the Ten Commandments. He memorized many other things as well.

When Michael was six, he went to school. Only boys went to school. The school was in the synagogue. Here, Michael learned to read the religious scrolls and to write. Michael's teacher was also a "chazan," or official of the synagogue.

Since Michael was a good student, he started to school at the academy when he was ten. (Some boys simply stopped going to school at the age of ten.) At the academy, Michael studied the Scriptures and Jewish history.

If Michael should keep doing well in his studies, he might be sent to study with a great rabbi. (Rabbi means "master" or "teacher.") Michael might even go and study in Jerusalem with the Sanhedrin.

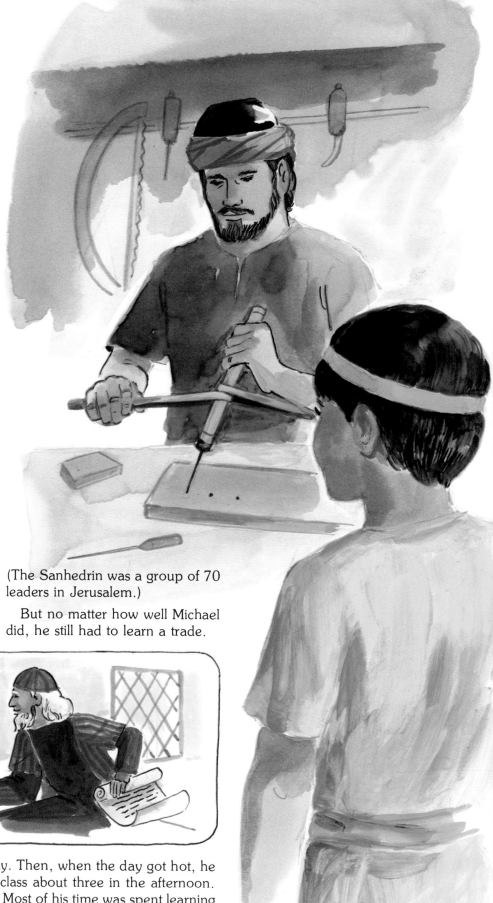

(The Sanhedrin was a group of 70 leaders in Jerusalem.)

But no matter how well Michael did, he still had to learn a trade.

Michael went to school early in the day. Then, when the day got hot, he could go home. He'd come again to class about three in the afternoon. The teacher made Michael work hard. Most of his time was spent learning Jewish history and law. Jewish people thought these were the most important things to learn.

Michael often went with his father to his carpentry shop. The shop was on a street filled with little booths for craftsmen and merchants.

Michael's father expected Michael to work hard. Michael already knew how to use the hammer and saw and axe. Now he was ready to work on a yoke for oxen.

Michael's father explained how to plane the wood to make it smooth. The yoke had to be planed until it was very smooth, so no splinters would hurt the oxen.

Michael's sister, Naomi, received all of her education from her mother. Naomi had learned to read. She knew many Scripture passages and Jewish laws and traditions. Her mother taught her how to make bread and how to sweep the house clean. Naomi could cook a fine stew. And she was learning to weave cloth.

Michael's friend, Peter, was learning to be a fisherman like his father. Not only could he use a line and hook, but he knew how to fish with a great net.

David, another of Michael's friends, was the son of a merchant. He sometimes went on buying trips with his father. This picture shows David helping to pack a camel.

23

Hard at Work

There were many ways to earn a living in Palestine. One of the most common in Capernaum was as a fisherman. Capernaum was right on the Sea of Galilee. The Sea of Galilee is a beautiful fresh-water lake, famous for its fish.

Fish from the Sea of Galilee were sent to Rome as special delicacies. Other fish were taken to Jerusalem for sale in the market near the Fish Gate. And, of course, many, many of the fish were sold right in Capernaum, almost as soon as they were caught.

Fishermen used small boats with sails on them. These boats also had oars. Most fishermen used large nets. These nets had weights all around the edges, as well as a drawstring.

A fisherman would throw the net out onto the water. The trick was to make the net land flat on the water. Then the weights would pull the edges down into the water. As the net sank, the fisherman would pull the drawstring, closing the net around any fish that were inside. Then he'd pull the net, with the fish inside, back into the boat.

Sometimes fishermen used an even larger net and pulled it between two boats. People also fished with a line and a hook, and sometimes with a spear.

Capernaum was a thriving town in New Testament times. It was a center for trade. Roman soldiers were stationed there. There were many ways to make a living in Capernaum. Besides those pictured, people could be traders or bankers, camel drivers, barbers, potters, goldsmiths, weavers, dyers, tax collectors, shoemakers, or blacksmiths.

Some people were merchants. They bought and sold goods. A merchant might specialize in just one kind of product. Or, he might sell many different products.

Every town needs physicians. So did Capernaum. While some of the physicians of the day were medical doctors, some were rabbis who gave medical advice.

There were many farmers in Galilee. Often, farmers lived in the villages or towns. They went out each day to work the land. Some owned their own farms.

Shepherds took care of sheep and, sometimes, goats. Shepherds would lead their flocks out into the wilderness to graze. Jesus spoke of a "Good Shepherd."

Some people were stone masons. Only the rich could afford houses of stone. But city and palace buildings were made of stone; and King Herod built lots of these.

Jesus' Friends Held These Jobs

Jesus Himself was a carpenter, as Joseph had been. Read Matthew 13:55.

Matthew, one of Jesus' disciples, was a tax collector. Read Matthew 9:9.

Peter, Andrew, James, and John, four of Jesus' disciples, were fishermen. Read Matthew 4:18-22.

We don't know what jobs the other disciples held.

The apostle Paul, who became an apostle after Jesus went back to Heaven, was a tent maker.

Paul's friends, Aquila and Priscilla, were tent makers too. Read Acts 18:2,3.

Lydia, an early Christian, was a seller of purple fabrics. Read Acts 16:14.

Luke, who wrote the book of Luke, was a physician.

The Work of Women

Women were the keepers of the house and the cooks. They were in charge of clothes and food for their families. They took care of the young children. If the family had animals, the women often fed and cared for them.

Women worked very hard in Palestine. Everything had to be done by hand.

One of their most pleasant jobs was going to get water. For, at the well, they could stop and visit with their friends. That was the fun part. The not-so-fun part was carrying the heavy jars of water back home on their heads.

Women spent much time cooking. They usually cooked two meals a day. They dried fruits and salted fish or meat to keep for later use. And they made bread every day.

Often, women made clothes. They spun wool or flax, then wove cloth, then made a coat or robe. Some women, if they were very skillful at weaving, even sold their cloth.

Women took care of the young children. Michael had learned much about the Scriptures from his mother. And women were their daughters' teachers.

Some women were midwives. They helped deliver babies. They nursed sick people and took care of them. Often, they knew a lot about healing herbs and other medicines.

Some women owned property. While it was unusual for a woman to own property, it was not unheard of. Proverbs tells of a woman who bought a vineyard.

Mary and Martha

Mary and Martha were good friends of Jesus. Often, He stayed at their house. One time when He came, Mary sat down to hear Jesus' teachings. Martha was very busy preparing a meal. Soon Martha complained to Jesus about Mary not helping her. Read Jesus' answer in Luke 10:38-42.

Fun for Michael

Children all over the world, and in all times, have found ways to have fun. In Michael's time, children must have had lots of ways to play. They certainly would have enjoyed running along the shore of the Sea of Galilee. Perhaps they searched there for beautiful, smooth stones.

Many children in Galilee learned to swim. Indeed, parents were supposed to teach their children to swim. Michael and his friends might have gone swimming in the Sea of Galilee.

There were plenty of hills nearby for rock climbing and exploring.

We don't know a lot about the games and other play activities of children in New Testament times. We do know that some children played with dolls. Archaeologists have found dolls and toy furniture. They also have found balls and dice and toy tools.

Some children got to ride on an ox as he walked round and round on a threshing floor. That would have been fun, for sure.

The Bible mentions that children in the market place sometimes played make-believe games. They pretended to be in a wedding, with some children playing pipes and others dancing. Or they pretended to be in a funeral procession, all mourning for the dead person. Often, there were long funeral processions, with professional mourners hired to weep and wail. Flute players sometimes played. A pretend procession would have been lots of fun.

Suppertime was usually a time of family fellowship and enjoyment. Jewish families were often close and loving, and the evening meal was a time of day when the entire family could be together.

Michael and his friends may have played a game with a ball. Archaeologists have found balls from the first century A.D. We don't know what kinds of games used balls in those days; but certainly Michael and his friends threw and caught the ball, just as children do today. And perhaps they bounced balls too.

Pets are always fun. Children in Michael's time must have liked animals as much as modern-day children do. Perhaps Michael had a pet lamb.

Michael probably liked to climb trees. He might have found a sycamore tree or a pine tree or an oak tree that was good for climbing.

Whether or not Michael was a good swimmer, he certainly would have liked to wade in the Sea of Galilee. Wading would have been a good way to cool off.

Capernaum—A Military Outpost

Capernaum was on the north-west shore of the Sea of Galilee. In Greek, the town was called Capernaum. In Hebrew, its name was Kefar Nahum, or "the village of Nahum." Capernaum was on a main highway that went through Galilee. This highway went from Jerusalem in the south to Damascus in the north.

The Romans had a garrison of soldiers at Capernaum. The garrison was led by a centurion. (A centurion was the leader of 100 soldiers.) Capernaum was an important trading city. From Damascus in the north came caravans of goods. Merchants came from Jerusalem in the south, and from the palaces and cities of Herod and, later, Herod's sons. A taxing place, or custom-house, was in Capernaum.

Capernaum was also an important fishing center. Many of the people who lived there were fishermen. Six days a week, the boats went out and returned, filled with fish.

An historian named Josephus, who lived in the first century, A.D., wrote about the area around Capernaum. Here is what he said. "Its nature is wonderful as well as its beauty; its soil is so fruitful that all sorts of trees grow upon it."

Jesus in Capernaum

Jesus spent much time in Capernaum. Peter lived there. Jesus may have made Peter's house His headquarters.

Jesus performed many miracles in Capernaum. He healed Peter's mother-in-law. Read Matthew 8:14, 15. He preached many times. He even preached in the synagogue. Capernaum is where Jesus said, "I am the bread of life."

Matthew called Capernaum Jesus' own city. Read Matthew 9:1.

Near Capernaum, Jesus called the four fishermen—Peter, Andrew, James, and John—to be disciples. Read Matthew 4:13, 18-22.

Also near Capernaum, Jesus called Matthew to be a disciple. Read Matthew 9:9.

Capernaum is only ruins now. The ruins are called Tel Hum. They stand in the shade of cyprus trees. Archaeologists have found olive presses, stone flour mills, and ovens in the ruins. There are pieces of tall columns. And there are the remains of a synagogue, built in about 200 A.D. This synagogue would not have been in Capernaum when Jesus was there. But people say it probably is built on the foundation of the synagogue in which Jesus preached.

Trip to Jerusalem

Twelve-year-old Michael and his family were busy at work. His mother sang while she worked. They were going to Jerusalem for the feast of the Passover.

Michael's father was loading the last bundle of food on the donkey.

Soon Michael and his family began their journey. They started south from Capernaum. (You can trace their journey on the map on page 33.)

It was almost a week's journey to Jerusalem. Michael and his family would walk around the Sea of Galilee on the west side. They would cross to the east of the Jordan River and follow the river south. They'd come back across the Jordan in Judea. They'd even get to see Jericho before they got to Jerusalem.

Michael and his family were not the only travelers on the road. Many, many people went to Jerusalem for this special feast. In fact, some Jews tried to get to Jerusalem twice, sometimes even three times, a year for the special feasts. The feasts were times of religious importance. But they were happy holidays, as well.

Michael and his family carried much of their food with them. There were no restaurants along the way. There were market places in cities, but nothing in between.

Michael and his family walked. They took turns carrying baby Matthew. Sometimes they let him ride in his pouch on the little donkey that carried their supplies.

Most nights on the journey, Michael and his family slept out in the open, under the stars. Michael liked that part best of all. The nights were so peaceful and quiet.

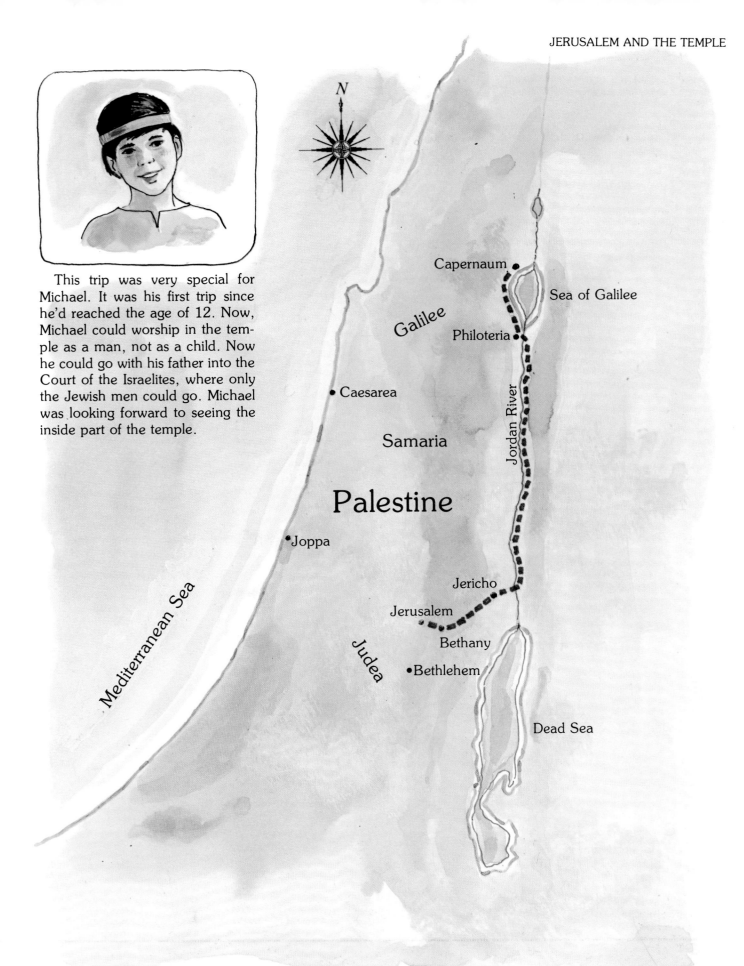

This trip was very special for Michael. It was his first trip since he'd reached the age of 12. Now, Michael could worship in the temple as a man, not as a child. Now he could go with his father into the Court of the Israelites, where only the Jewish men could go. Michael was looking forward to seeing the inside part of the temple.

N

Capernaum

Sea of Galilee

Galilee

Philoteria

Caesarea

Jordan River

Samaria

Palestine

Joppa

Jericho

Jerusalem

Bethany

Judea

Bethlehem

Mediterranean Sea

Dead Sea

Jerusalem

Michael and his family stood on the Mount of Olives. "Look!" Michael called. "There they are! See—the walls of Jerusalem!"

Sure enough, just below, they could see the holy city, the place of the beautiful temple. Michael was so excited, he ran on ahead. Across the Valley of the Kidron he ran, and to the gate of the city itself. Then back Michael ran, to join his family and the other pilgrims.

The pilgrims were singing a psalm, a psalm they often sang as they approached the city. "I was glad when they said unto me, Let us go into the house of the Lord. Our feet shall stand within thy gates, O Jerusalem."

Mount of Olives — Michael and his family could see Jerusalem from here.

hippodrome

bridge

temple

bridge

Antonia Fortress

second wall

One of the things Michael saw in Jerusalem was Psephinus' Tower. It was over 100 feet tall. From that tower, on clear days, people could see the Mediterranean Sea.

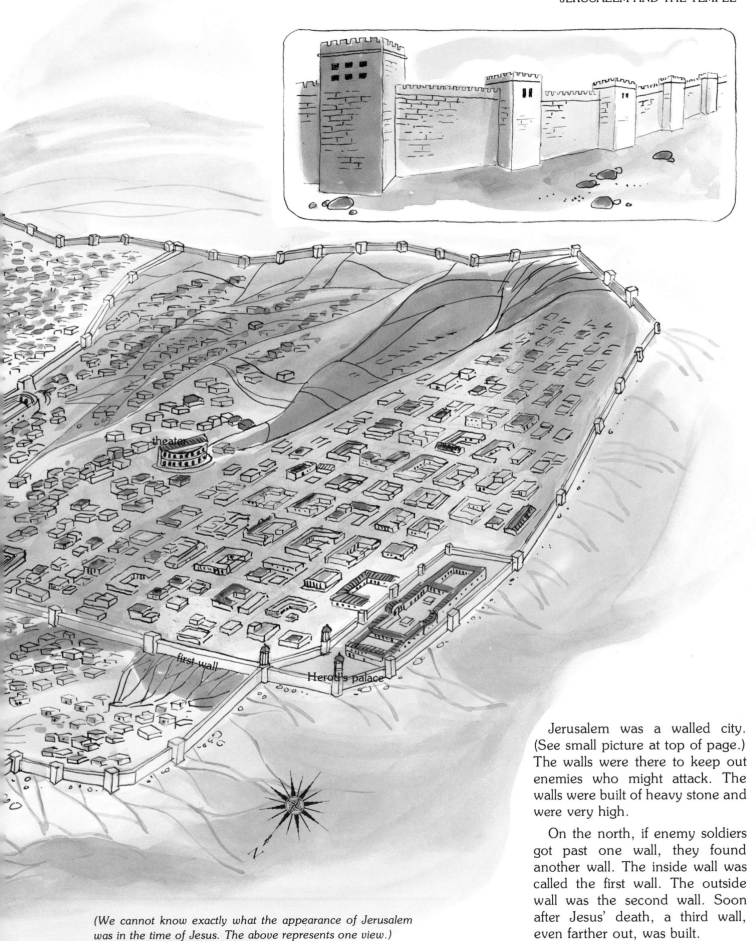

theater

first wall

Herod's palace

(We cannot know exactly what the appearance of Jerusalem was in the time of Jesus. The above represents one view.)

Jerusalem was a walled city. (See small picture at top of page.) The walls were there to keep out enemies who might attack. The walls were built of heavy stone and were very high.

On the north, if enemy soldiers got past one wall, they found another wall. The inside wall was called the first wall. The outside wall was the second wall. Soon after Jesus' death, a third wall, even farther out, was built.

35

Michael in Jerusalem

"Your mother and Naomi and Matthew are visiting with your aunt, Mary," said Michael's father. "So, you and I will tour Jerusalem.

"Jerusalem is a very old city," Michael's father continued. As he and Michael walked through narrow streets, he told Michael of the history of Jerusalem. "We think that people first built a city here because of the natural spring, the Gihon. It comes out of the hill near Jerusalem.

"A long, long time ago, our ancestor, Abraham, met Melchizedek, who was the priest-king of this city. Then the city was called Salem.

"In the time of our judges, Israelites held the land around it, but not Jerusalem itself.

"David captured Jerusalem and made it his royal city. And he built a fortress inside the city. He called the fort Zion. That's why the whole area is now called Mount Zion."

"Where was that fortress?" Michael asked.

"No one knows," said his father. "It isn't here anymore. David's city was much smaller than Jerusalem is now.

"Long after King David's time, Hezekiah built the tunnel that brought the waters from Gihon underground to the city. Because he did that, the Assyrian king, Sennacherib, couldn't conquer Jerusalem. But, of course, Nebuchadnezzar, a later king of Babylon, did capture us."

"Yes," said Michael, "and then King Cyrus let us come back."

Below are pictures of some things Michael and his father saw.

Three Towers Built by Herod

Phasael Tower

Hippicus Tower

Mariamne Tower

Herod the Great built three towers very close together. He built them to protect his palace. They are the Phasael Tower, the Hippicus Tower, and the Mariamne Tower.

The Phasael Tower was named after Herod's brother, Phasael. It was about 135 feet high. The Hippicus Tower was named after a friend of Herod. It was about 120 feet high. Water was stored in its base. The Mariamne Tower was named after Herod's queen, even though he had her killed. The Mariamne Tower was 74 feet high.

THE MONUMENT OF HYRCANUS was a tomb. John Hyrcanus, a Jewish king, was buried in this tomb. John Hyrcanus ruled between Old and New Testament times.

WOOD MARKET. Wood was stored and sold outside the walls of Jerusalem. No one wanted all that wood inside, because it might catch fire.

BRIDGE. Two bridges crossed from the temple area to the upper city area. They crossed over the Tyropean Valley. Herod built one of them; the Hasmoneans, the other.

THE HASMONEAN PALACE was built across from the temple. The palace had two towers, with a building between. The Hasmoneans ruled before the time of Jesus.

THEATER. Herod the Great built a theater, for plays. It was an open-air theater. The seats were stone steps in a semi-circle around the stage. The Greeks and Romans greatly enjoyed plays. Sometimes the theater was used for large gatherings of other kinds, as well. Many of the Jews hated the theater. It was Roman!

One part of Herod's temple is still standing today. It is part of the wall that was all around the temple area. It is the southwestern corner of that wall. Its foundation may be even older than Herod's temple.

Now it is called the Wailing Wall. For centuries, people have come to the wall to pray, and to mourn for friends and family members who have died.

More About Jerusalem

Jerusalem had many pools for water storage. Judea had little rainfall, and water was precious.

One of the most important of the pools was the Pool of Siloam. In New Testament times, this pool probably was fed from the spring, Gihon. The spring was the most important water supply in Jerusalem.

WATER GATE. A gate called the Water Gate stood near one of the pools. This gate was in the wall around Jerusalem. There were other gates, as well.

Pool of Bethesda

Another important pool was the Pool of Bethesda. This pool also was fed from a spring. Around the pool were five large porches.

People thought an angel came to this pool, to trouble the waters. Often, the five porches were filled with sick people waiting to get into the water. Jesus healed a man here.

SHEEP MARKET. Sheep were often sacrificed in the temple. So there were sheep markets, where people could buy animals for sacrifices.

HIPPODROME. The Hippodrome was a sports stadium that Herod the Great built. The Romans held chariot races there. It had one straight end and one round end.

ANTONIA FORTRESS. After Herod the Great became king, he rebuilt an old fortress at the corner of the temple area. It was called the Antonia Fortress. It was named after Mark Antony, a famous Roman. A stairway connected it to the temple. It looked like a palace. Some Jews hated having it so close to the temple.

Jesus in Jerusalem

Mary and Joseph took Jesus to Jerusalem when He was 40 days old. When He was 12 years old, they took Him to Jerusalem again. Jesus may have been to Jerusalem many more times in His childhood.

As an adult, Jesus often came to Jerusalem. The first year of His ministry, He cleansed the temple. This was at the time of Passover. John 2:13-17 tells of this incident. The second year, He healed a man at Passover time. Read John 5:1-9.

The third year, Jesus was in and out of Jerusalem several times. He came for the feast of Tabernacles. He traveled in secret, for some Jewish leaders wanted to kill Him. Read John 7:1-13.

Later, Jesus came to Jerusalem again. Read John 10:22-39.

Then, in the fourth and last year of His ministry, Jesus came to Jerusalem for the feast of the Passover. He spent the last week of His earthly life in and near Jerusalem. The pictures and map tell of that last week.

TRIUMPHAL ENTRY. Jesus rode into Jerusalem in triumph. He rode on a donkey, and people lined up to see Him. They shouted, "Hosanna to the son of David."

CLEANSING OF THE TEMPLE. In the temple's outer court, Jesus found people selling, changing money, and cheating. This made Jesus angry. He threw out the cheaters.

LAST SUPPER. Jesus and His disciples used an upper room of a house for their celebration of the Passover. During the traditional Passover meal, Jesus started a new tradition. "Remember Me," He said, "when you eat the bread and drink the wine." To this day, Christians observe the Lord's Supper, as Jesus commanded.

GARDEN OF GETHSEMANE. Jesus went out of Jerusalem to the Garden of Gethsemane, to pray. Here, Judas brought Jesus' enemies to capture Jesus.

PALACE OF CAIAPHAS. Jesus was taken to the palace of the high priest, Caiaphas. Jesus was kept here until daybreak. Here, Peter denied Jesus three times.

BEFORE PILATE. The Jews condemned Jesus, then took Him to Pilate. Only Pilate could order death. Pilate sent Jesus to Herod Antipas.

HEROD'S PALACE. Herod Antipas questioned Jesus and made fun of Him. Then Herod sent Jesus back to Pilate. Pilate finally condemned Jesus to death on a cross.

CRUCIFIXION. On Calvary, Jesus was crucified. Calvary was a hill outside the city wall. No one is sure which hill it was. It may have been the place shown on the map. Jesus died that day. While He was on the cross, a great darkness came. An earthquake shook the city and tore apart the veil of the temple. Three days later, Jesus rose from the dead.

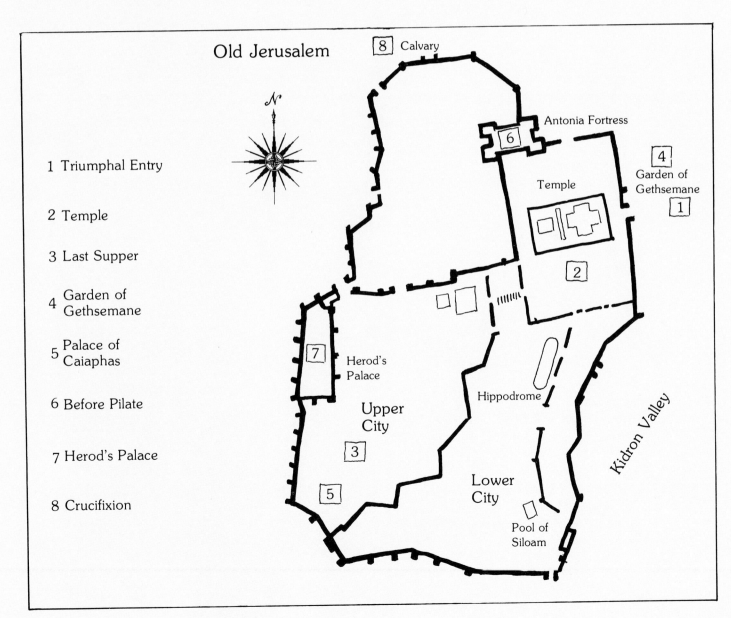

Old Jerusalem

1 Triumphal Entry

2 Temple

3 Last Supper

4 Garden of Gethsemane

5 Palace of Caiaphas

6 Before Pilate

7 Herod's Palace

8 Crucifixion

8 Calvary

Antonia Fortress

6

4
Garden of Gethsemane
1

Temple

2

7
Herod's Palace

Upper City

3

Hippodrome

5

Lower City

Pool of Siloam

Kidron Valley

41

Going to the Temple

Michael and his family were going to the temple. They walked up some stairs. As they walked, they sang David's psalm: "Who shall ascend into the hill of the Lord? or who shall stand in his holy place? He that hath clean hands, and a pure heart."

Soon they were at the Huldah gates. Beyond was the Royal Porch. From this porch, with all its columns, they could see the outer court, or the Court of the Gentiles. To the right was another porch, Solomon's Porch.

All around the court, Michael could see the columns Herod had built. Soon Michael and his family were in the outer court. Above, the sky was a bright blue. People thronged in the outer court. They had come from all over the country for the Passover feast.

This picture shows the outer court around the temple. All people were allowed to come into the outer court. But only Jews could climb the steps and go inside.

In the outer court, merchants sold doves for sacrifices. Money changers exchanged Roman money for Jewish money.

All around the outer court were open porches, with pillars and with roofs overhead.

Jesus and the Temple

Early in His career, Jesus cleansed the temple. Read John 2:13-17. He came often to the temple to speak. The writers of the Gospels tell about many of Jesus' teachings at the temple. Read John 8.

John says Jesus' teachings made people so angry they wanted to stone Jesus.

Mark tells what Jesus said about the poor widow who brought her tiny offering to the temple. Read Mark 12:41-44.

After Jesus' triumphal entry and His second cleansing of the temple, some children were still praising Jesus and shouting, "Hosanna to the son of David." The priests and scribes were already angry at Jesus for stopping their money-making schemes. The shouting and praising by the children made them even more angry. Read Matthew 21:1-17.

The porch on the south was called the Royal Porch. It was from this porch that Michael and his family viewed the area. The picture shows what they would have seen.

The porch in the background would be Solomon's Porch. It was on the east side of the temple.

43

More About the Temple

Michael and his family walked across the outer court of the temple toward a raised area on which were other courts, as well as the temple proper. As they came closer, Michael saw the signs that said Gentiles must not go any farther. Only Jews could go up the steps, through the rail, into the sacred enclosure.

Before going into this section, Michael and his family walked around the outer court. From time to time, Michael's father would look around, as if in wonder.

Michael knew how important the temple was to his parents.

The temple walls around the outer court were strong, as strong as fortress walls, with towers like fortress towers. King Herod the Great had rebuilt the temple when he became king. So, now, it was called Herod's temple, at least by some people. Michael's father never called it that. Michael's father called it the temple of the Lord God Jehovah.

The temple was the center of Jewish religious life. It held Jewish people together in worship of God.

Michael heard his father speaking a psalm, and joined in. "Bless ye the Lord, all ye servants of the Lord, which by night stand in the house of the Lord. Lift up your hands in the sanctuary, and bless the Lord."

Soon Michael and his family decided to leave the Court of Gentiles, or outer court, and go into the Court of Women in the sacred enclosure. To do so, they went up some steps and passed through a gate.

The Gate to the Women's Court was very ornate. Michael loved to look at its patterns. The gate was covered with gold.

Women's Court

All Jews were allowed to come into the Women's Court. It was called the Women's Court because women couldn't go any farther inside. Like the outer court, the Women's Court had no roof.

When the widow gave her mite to God, she was in the Women's Court. She might have put her coin in one of the trumpet-shaped offering boxes.

NAZIRITES. One of the corner sections inside the Women's Court was reserved for Nazirites. These were people taking special religious vows. They didn't cut their hair.

LEPERS. Lepers used one of the corner sections. Lepers had a bad skin disease. They couldn't be around other people once it was discovered that they had leprosy. But sometimes other diseases looked like leprosy. People with these other diseases sometimes got well. Then they had to come to the priests, so the priests could perform a special cleansing ceremony.

Gate Into the Court of the Israelites

Michael looked at the gate that led to the Court of the Israelites. It was incredibly beautiful.

Tomorrow morning, for the first time, Michael would go with his father through that gate. His father had promised they would come for the early morning worship.

There were rounded steps leading up to the gate. Right now, Levites stood on the steps singing and playing lyres, trumpets, and other instruments, in praise to the Lord God. The sound made Michael feel wonderful!

Since Passover was near, the Levites sang, "Sing aloud unto God our strength: make a joyful noise unto the God of Jacob. Take a psalm, and bring hither the timbrel, the pleasant harp with the psaltery. Blow up the trumpet in the new moon, in the time appointed, on our solemn feast day."

Musical Instruments

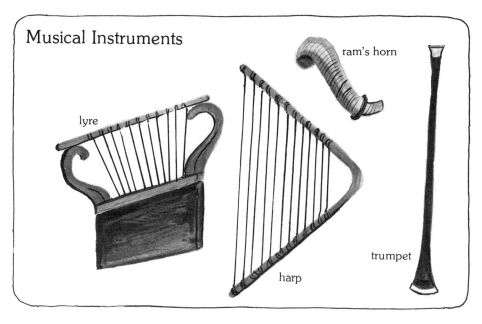

lyre

ram's horn

harp

trumpet

In the Court of the Israelites

Early the next morning, while it was still dark, Michael and his father walked to the temple. Quietly, they walked through the outer court, through the Women's Court, and into the Court of the Israelites.

Here is where the Jewish men came for worship. Just inside was the Court of the Priests. It contained a big altar on which animal sacrifices were offered. The altar was made from unhewn stones, was about 48 feet square at its base, and between 20 and 30 feet high. It was made up of different layers, each one smaller than the one before. The top part, the spot on which the animals were burned, was about 36 feet square. A sloping ramp on the south side of the altar allowed the priests to climb to its top.

"Out of the depths, I cry to thee, O Lord!" The voice of the priest, in the stillness of the morning, startled Michael. "Lord, hear my voice! My soul waits for the Lord more than watchmen for the morning."

Now began the sacrifice. Levites brought lambs for the priests to examine. When the lambs were approved, they were sacrificed on the altar.

All this time, priests stood near the altar. They blessed the worshipers in the name of Jehovah.

Then cymbals clanged, and priests blew silver trumpets.

Next, Levites read a psalm and a part of the Law. Other Levites played on musical instruments as the Scripture was read. The Levites would read a verse, then the priests would blow the trumpets, and the worshipers would bow and pray. The Levites would read another verse, then the priests would blow the trumpets, and the worshipers would bow and pray.

Michael listened carefully to all that was read, and bowed with his father each time, praying silently.

When the service was over, Michael and his father walked outside.

"What a great way to start the day!" Michael said to his father.

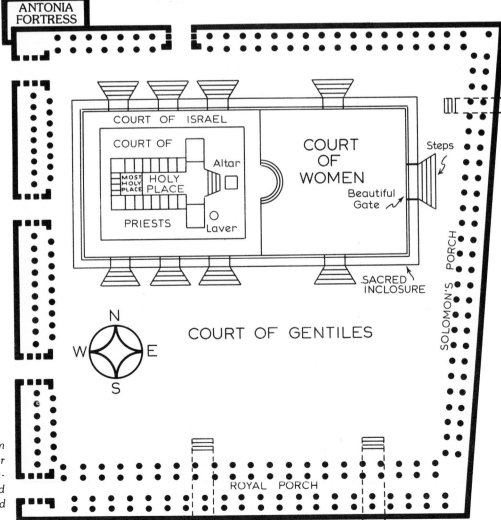

Chart taken from "New Training for Service," published by Standard Publishing. Used by permission.

Places of Worship

As Michael went to the temple each morning and evening, he learned about worship; he prayed to God and thought about God's goodness to Israel.

In the early days, God's people had used an altar in their worship. The altar was a symbol. It meant, "Here is a place of worship."

An altar reminded Abel of God's gift of life. It reminded Noah of God's protection during the flood. An altar reminded Abraham of God's test of his faith.

An altar

Altars were made of many materials. Some were simply a pile of stones, or perhaps just one stone. Others were elaborate. Altars were different shapes and sizes.

The tabernacle

During the Israelites' long journey in the wilderness, the people worshiped in a beautiful tent called the tabernacle. The Israelites moved the tabernacle when they moved.

After many years, a permanent place of worship was built. This was Solomon's temple—beautiful! Spectacular! The temple was exactly twice as large as the tabernacle had been. It was 90-feet long, 30-feet wide, and 45-feet high. It was located in an open court. Builders put together its stones and its carved wood without ax or hammer. They decorated the temple with gleaming gold. Still the basic pattern of the temple was the same as that of the tabernacle. Its purpose was the same, too.

Solomon's temple stood for over 350 years. Then Nebuchadnezzar, a Babylonian king, conquered Judah. He destroyed Solomon's temple on Mount Zion and burned Jerusalem. Nebuchadnezzar took the young and the healthy captive. Seventy years of sadness and repentance followed. The Israelites turned back to God. In their sorrow, they sang this psalm: "By the rivers of Babylon, there we sat down, yea, we wept. . . . How shall we sing the Lord's song in a strange land?" (Psalm 137:1, 4).

In Babylon, the Israelites met together in small groups. They prayed and heard the reading of God's Word. Their meeting places were the first synagogues.

Then a great Persian king, Cyrus, overthrew Babylon. Cyrus allowed the Jews to return to their homeland. The temple the Jews rebuilt was even larger than Solomon's. When Herod the Great became king, he rebuilt the temple a third time. This picture of Herod's temple shows the entrance to the holy place. Within the holy place was the Holy of Holies.

Herod's temple lasted until 70 A.D. Then the Roman conquerer, Titus, destroyed it, with all of Jerusalem.

Laws and Customs

As Michael and his father returned to Aunt Mary's house, Father asked, "What is the beginning of wisdom?"

Michael knew the answer. "To fear and love God, and to obey all of His laws."

Michael was 12 years old. He knew much about Jewish law.

Jewish laws gave the world many important ideas. These are a few.

1. In Israel, even a slave had rights.

2. A worker deserved payment for his labor, and should be paid promptly.

3. Many of Israel's political leaders were chosen because of ability, not ancestry.

4. In Israel, people who caused damages to other people were required to make payment.

5. There had to be two witnesses to a crime. The accused person had the right to a fair trial.

6. Israelites believed kindness should be shown to the poor and to the helpless.

7. They thought of women as helpers, not as slaves or property.

Every farmer was to leave one corner of each field unharvested. This was so poor people could help themselves. Do you remember how this law helped Ruth?

You shall have no other Gods before me.

You shall not make for yourself an idol.

You shall not misuse the name of the Lord your God.

Remember the Sabbath day by keeping it holy.

Honor your father and your mother.

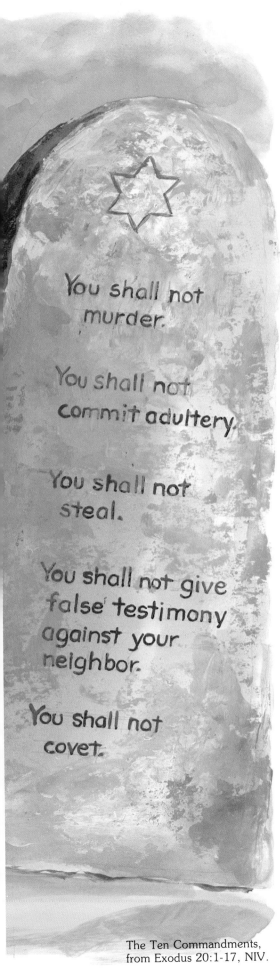

You shall not murder.

You shall not commit adultery.

You shall not steal.

You shall not give false testimony against your neighbor.

You shall not covet.

The Ten Commandments, from Exodus 20:1-17, NIV.

SACRIFICES. As God had commanded, people brought animals to be sacrificed. The animals had to be perfect, not lame or sick. People also brought wheat or grapes or other crops. There were three reasons for sacrifices: 1. In repentance, and for forgiveness of sins. 2. As a gift to God, in thanksgiving for His blessings. 3. As a way of communicating with God. Many families raised their own animals. Others bought them.

OFFERINGS. The people brought a part (called a tithe) of their earnings to God. They brought special offerings at special times. Also, they brought offerings for the poor. In the temple, there were 13 different chests with openings shaped like trumpets. Each one was for a different kind of offering.

Jesus and the Law

When asked what the greatest law was, Jesus said, " 'Love the Lord your God with all your heart and with all your soul and with all your mind.' This is the first and greatest commandment. And the second is like it: 'Love your neighbor as yourself.' All the Law and the Prophets hang on these two commandments." (Matthew 22:37-40, NIV).

The Sabbath

The day of the week Michael loved most was the Sabbath, day of joy and gladness.

The Sabbath was a day when members of a family felt especially close to each other and to God. The Scriptures commanded: "This day is sacred to the Lord your God. Do not mourn or weep. . . . Go and enjoy choice food and sweet drinks, and send some to those who have nothing prepared" (Nehemiah 8:9, 10, NIV).

The Sabbath began at sunset on Friday night. As darkness fell, Michael's mother lit the Sabbath lamp. She crossed her hands above the light as she said, "Blessed art Thou, O Lord our God, king of the world, who has sanctified us by Thy commandments and commanded us to kindle Sabbath lights."

When Father came home from the service at the synagogue, he gave his blessing. The family went through a hand-washing ceremony, then ate the Sabbath meal.

Michael and has family went to Saturday morning worship in the synagogue. The synagogue stood on the highest ground in the village.

The men and boys always sat together on one side. The women and girls sat on the other side.

After the worship time, the family ate the noontime Sabbath meal. Families visited one another in the afternoon, then went to a late afternoon worship service at the synagogue. Finally, there was another Sabbath meal at home.

The Sabbath was a day of rest. All work was forbidden. Michael's mother couldn't cook. So, usually, she worked all day Friday to get ready for the Sabbath.

On the Sabbath, people were not allowed to carry burdens or travel very far. On the Sabbath, no one discussed business. People did not buy or sell goods.

Food Rules

Michael knew exactly what to eat and what not to eat. He had been taught carefully.

The Scriptures contained laws, which his family observed. Observing the laws helped to keep food sanitary in the hot climate. There were no refrigerators then.

Jewish people could eat fish with scales and fins, and some birds. They could eat locusts, grasshoppers, and beetles. But the only four-legged animals Jews could eat were those that chewed their cuds and had cloven hoofs. (A cloven hoof is a hoof split in two. Animals that chew their cuds eat grass and other vegetable matter.)

Jewish people never ate meat from predators. (Predators are animals that eat other animals.)

Special laws governed the way the people prepared meat. When animals were killed, their blood had to be drained from them immediately. (Today, "kosher" food is prepared this way, and then approved by a rabbi.)

Also, people were not allowed to eat meat that had been sacrificed to an idol.

Michael's family would never have eaten pork. Pigs do not chew their cuds. Pigs were sometimes raised in Palestine, but they were sold to Romans and other foreigners.

The cook could not boil a young goat in its mother's milk. Even today, many Jewish people will not eat a dish that has both meat and milk in it. Some Jews today separate dishes, silverware, pots, and utensils into two sets. One set is for cooking and serving meat; the other set is for milk and milk products.

Uncleanness and Sickness

Sickness and handicaps were common in New Testament times. While some people lived to an old age, many died young. And they died of diseases that doctors today know how to control. Today, people have better medicines. And they know how to get rid of sewage better, thus improving health.

The Scriptures gave rules for cleanliness, and the Jewish people followed them carefully. Jews washed their hands before every meal. This was done for two reasons. First, since people ate many foods with their hands, they needed clean hands. Second, the Jews washed their hands before every holy act. Praying was a holy act, and they prayed before eating.

There also was a foot-washing custom. When people came into Michael's house, Michael or his sister washed their feet. People wore sandals; the roads were dusty; the feet needed washing.

If people handled dead animals, they bathed very carefully afterward. Or if they had been around a sick person, they bathed carefully. The Scriptural rules for cleanliness helped keep people healthy.

Jesus, the Healer

While Jesus was on earth, He performed many healing miracles. One of the reasons people came to see Him and then followed Him was His kindness.

Jesus healed blind people and people who couldn't speak or hear. Jesus also healed crippled people.

Lepers came to Jesus to be healed and went away singing because they were well.

Others Jesus healed included a paralyzed man and a woman who couldn't stop bleeding.

Some of the people Jesus healed were children. Three stories about children are told in John 4:46-53; Matthew 9:18-26; and Mark 7:25 30.

The most dread disease of the ancient world was leprosy. People were not allowed to touch a person with leprosy. Lepers had to live apart from healthy people.

Death and Burial

One day Michael asked, "What is the most unclean thing a person can touch?"

"Probably a dead body," said his father. "There are very strict rules for people who have touched a dead body. They must wash themselves and their clothes. Even then, they are unclean for seven days."

"Isn't that hard on the people who have to take care of dead bodies?" asked Michael.

"Yes," said his father. "But it's part of caring for the dead. We mourn when a person dies, and we never leave the body unattended. We bury the body before night on the same day a person dies."

"Do you remember the story about Abraham?" Michael's father asked. "The story of his buying the cave of Machpelah?"

"Yes," said Michael. "He bought it so he could bury Sarah in it."

"That's right. That cave was used for many generations. It is still in existence." (Read the story in Genesis 23:1-20.)

In early days, the Jews dug out and enlarged natural caves to make burial places. These were called sepulchres. However, as the years went by and more burial places were needed, Jewish people began to use cemeteries. All burying places were at least 80 feet from a city wall. No one was ever buried inside a city.

To prepare a body for burial, people washed it carefully. They placed sweet-smelling spices on it. Then they wrapped it in long, linen cloths.

Mourners were loud and unrestrained in their weeping and wailing. Making noise and crying was their way of showing how much the person had been loved.

Friends placed the body on a mat, or bier. Then four friends, one at each corner of the mat, carried the body. Usually, there was a procession to the grave.

People formed a funeral procession as soon as the body was prepared. First came the paid mourners, singing a dirge (funeral song) and beating a drum. Then came the bier with the body. The actual mourners—family, relatives, friends, and neighbors—came last. The body was placed in the tomb or grave. The door of the tomb was closed or the grave was covered.

When Jesus Died

When Jesus was dying on the cross, the Jews were anxious to have His body buried before the Sabbath began. Read John 19:31.

Near Calvary, there was a garden. In it was a tomb, never used. Joseph of Arimathea asked Pilate for Jesus' body, so he could bury it in the tomb. Read John 19:38-42.

Feasts and Holy Days

Passover

The Passover feast was beginning. Michael, his family, and his Aunt Mary's and Uncle Thomas' family gathered together.

"Now!" Michael whispered to his little cousin.

"What does the feast mean?" asked the cousin. Being the youngest child who could talk, he had been chosen to ask.

His father answered: "When we were slaves in Egypt, God told the Egyptians, 'Let my people go.' But the Egyptians refused. So God sent disasters or plagues. Still, the Egyptians refused. Then God sent the worst plague. Every first-born child of the Egyptians died.

"But the Israelites' children were spared. Here is how. Each Israelite family was told to kill a lamb and smear its blood on the doorposts and over the door. When God would see the blood, he would *pass over* that house.

"The Israelites did as God commanded; then they roasted the lambs. Wearing cloaks and sandals, they ate lamb with bitter herbs and unleavened bread. They held their staffs, ready to go. For soon, they would leave Egypt.

"To this day," the father continued, "during Passover, we kill a lamb and roast it. We eat it with bitter herbs and unleavened bread. We eat standing, cloaks and sandals on, staffs in our hands. We remember the night the angel passed over."

Later, Michael's father said, "The Passover is one of our major feasts. There are two other major ones — Pentecost and Tabernacles. And there are some lesser feasts, besides holy days."

Feast of Weeks

Another name for the feast of Weeks was "Pentecost." "Pente" means 50. This celebration came 50 days after the feast of Passover. The feast of Weeks was held to celebrate the winter wheat harvest. It was a time of gladness and joy. Each family brought two loaves of bread to the temple as an offering, in gratitude for the harvest.

Feast of Trumpets

Day of Atonement

The Day of Atonement was held five days before the feast of Tabernacles (see below). Its purpose was to bring the people back to a good relationship with God. First, the High Priest had to make atonement for himself and his family, then for the place of worship, then for all the Jewish people. Two goats were used. One was sacrificed; some of its blood was sprinkled in the most sacred part of the temple to make atonement for sin. The other goat was a scapegoat. The sins of the people were confessed over its head; then it was taken into a desert place and set free.

The feast of Trumpets marked the beginning of a civil new year. It was celebrated in the synagogues of every village and town. All day, people blew horns and trumpets. There were sacrifices in the temple. Everywhere, people prayed and chanted and sang. The new year began on the new moon in the month of Tishri, our October.

Feast of Tabernacles

One of the happiest celebrations of the year was the feast of Tabernacles, or "Ingathering." At this feast, people celebrated the harvest of all kinds of growing things. Best of all, people stayed in booths built of tree branches!

To a boy like Michael, the feast of Tabernacles was a "camping out" time. The grown-ups, though, spoke of the days when the Israelites had no homes at all. Instead, they had wandered in the desert and lived like nomads for 40 years.

57

Weddings and Parties

Michael was too young to wonder about what girl he would marry. Probably, though, a man in Capernaum was thinking, "Michael will make a good husband for my daughter."

When a young man was old enough to marry, his parents would choose a young woman for him. Often, the young man suggested the woman he would like to marry. The young man and young woman both had to consent to the marriage. However, seldom did either refuse to consent. Both took it for granted that their parents would choose well for them. The parents would send a friend to the father of the girl to suggest marriage.

The promise to marry was sacred to Jewish people. It was almost as difficult to break an engagement as it was to get a divorce.

The wedding feast was a long and happy party. Sometimes, the feast lasted for days. When invited to a wedding, people tried to go. It was a great insult not to go.

Early in Jesus' ministry, He was invited to a wedding feast. Jesus' mother was there also. At the feast, the people ran out of wine. Jesus' mother asked Him to help. Jesus changed water to wine, so the hosts wouldn't be embarrassed. (Read the story of this wedding in John 2:1-11.)

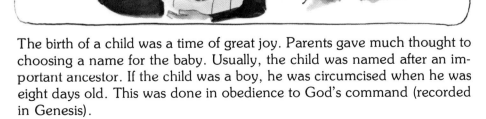

The birth of a child was a time of great joy. Parents gave much thought to choosing a name for the baby. Usually, the child was named after an important ancestor. If the child was a boy, he was circumcised when he was eight days old. This was done in obedience to God's command (recorded in Genesis).

It was a great privilege to have company. The host, or his children or servants, would wash a guest's feet and anoint his head with sweet-smelling oil.

Religious and Political Groups

One day, at the temple, Michael saw two men arguing. "Why are they arguing?" he asked his father.

"One is a Pharisee," said his father. "The other is a Sadducee. They are arguing about whether or not there is life after death."

Michael and his father walked closer to listen. The two men seemed glad to have an audience.

The Pharisees and Sadducees were important groups in New Testament times. They and some other important groups are described below.

PRIESTS. Priests were the descendants of Aaron, Moses' brother. These men conducted worship and made sacrifices at the temple.

LEVITES. Aaron had been a member of the tribe of Levi. So the tribe of Levi was known as the priestly tribe. Levites were given the job of helping the priests. As part of their help, Levites took care of the temple grounds, kept the supplies that were needed, acted as teachers, and were the musicians at the temple.

PHARISEES. Pharisees were a religious group who set themselves apart as "more righteous" than others. They followed the Mosaic law and the traditions of the elders—to the letter. Included among the Pharisees were some Levites and priests. Many of the Pharisees were hypocrites. (That means they were not as good as they pretended to be.)

SADDUCEES. The Sadducees were a religious sect that denied the existence of angels and life after death. Most were wealthy. Many of the priests in Jesus' time were Sadducees. The Sadducees were similar to a political party. They severely persecuted the early church.

ZEALOTS. Zealots were a fanatical group that wanted to be free of Roman rule. The Zealots assassinated people and tried to start rebellions.

Jesus and the Religious Leaders

Most of the religious leaders in Palestine did not believe Jesus was the Messiah. Jesus criticized them strongly. Read Matthew 23:1-36.

One leader, Nicodemus, once came to Jesus at night. He also defended Jesus against the other leaders. Read John 3:1-21 and John 7:50-52.

The more Jesus preached and taught, the more most religious leaders hated Him. Finally, the religious leaders decided Jesus must die. Read Matthew 26:3-5.

They captured Jesus and brought Him to trial. Read Matthew 26:47-67. They demanded that Jesus die.

Joseph of Arimathea, an important leader, gave a tomb, in which Jesus was buried. Nicodemus also helped to bury Jesus. Read John 19:38-40.

HERODIANS. The Herodians were a political party, giving devotion to the ruling family. Herod the Great encouraged this party and rewarded the Herodians for supporting him. His son, Herod Antipas, continued this practice.

ESSENES. The Essenes were a sect in Palestine. They went out into the wilderness to live by themselves. They lived very simply and shared their belongings with one another. They were careful students of the Scriptures.

THE SANHEDRIN. The Sanhedrin was the Jewish supreme court. There were 70 members, plus the president. The high priest was the president. There were Pharisees and Sadducees in the Sanhedrin. Many of the members were from important Jewish families. The Sanhedrin judged matters of law. It also decided on religious matters.

SCRIBES were the people who copied the Scriptures. All copying was done by hand. The scribes were careful to keep the handmade copies accurate. Scribes were highly honored. People greeted them respectfully and gave them seats of honor in the synagogues and at the feasts.

Judea

Michael thought of his land as God's promised land.

The Romans thought of the land in a different way. To them, Pontius Pilate (a Roman governor) ruled over one part of what had been Herod the Great's kingdom. This part included Judea and Samaria. Herod Antipas, Herod the Great's son, ruled over Galilee.

When Michael went to Jerusalem and stood on the Mount of Olives, much of what he saw was Judea. To the west, he saw beautiful, terraced farms on rounded hills. To the east, the land was more barren, sloping down to the Jordan River and the Dead Sea.

In winter, Judea had rain and the crops grew well. In summer, the land became hot and dry.

From Jerusalem, people could travel south to Bethlehem, or north to Bethel. If they wanted to go to the harbor city of Joppa, on the Mediterranean Sea, they went northwest about 30 miles.

Joppa was an important harbor.

There had been a city at Joppa long before the Israelites came. People said that Joppa meant "beauty." When the sun shone, the buildings in Joppa reflected a mass of great light. Today, this city is called Jaffa.

Another ancient city in Judea was Jericho. In New Testament times, the road from Jerusalem to Jericho was steep and perilous. People feared it, for robbers sometimes hid along the road and attacked travelers.

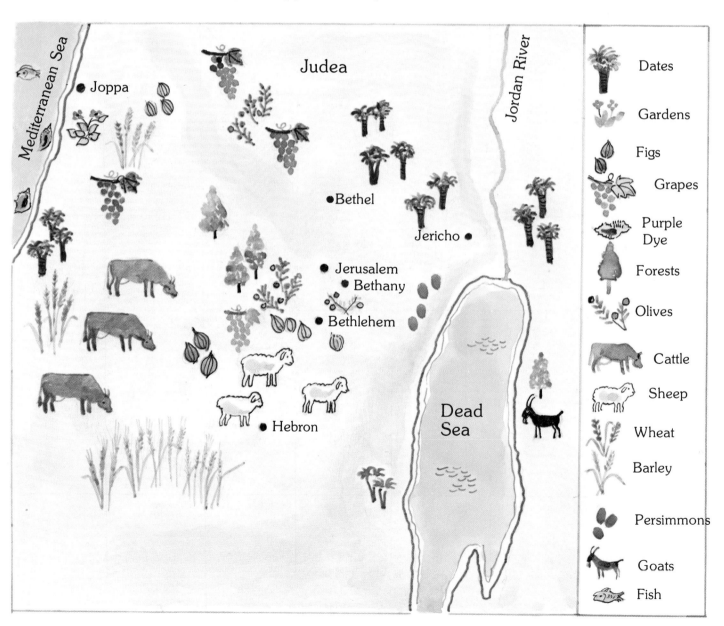

FIGS grew in Judea. They were an important crop in Bible times. People ate them fresh, made fig cakes out of them, or dried them for later use.

The hills of Judea were just right for growing grapes. Everywhere on the hills, Michael saw vineyards, some with fences around them. Some grapes grew along stone walls that kept the vines up off the ground. Near a vineyard there would be a wine press. Many vineyards also had watchtowers. Guards stood in the towers, in order to keep away thieves.

DATES also were grown in Judea. Dates grow on date palm trees. Some other food crops were wheat, barley, melons, cucumbers, and pomegranates.

OLIVES were an important crop, for from them came olive oil. People picked the olives very carefully. Then they pressed the olives to extract the oil.

Some people in Judea raised sheep, both for their own use and to sell. Sheep were used for food, and their wool was used to make clothing. People also raised cattle.

Jesus in Judea

Jesus taught in Judea early in His ministry. Read John 3:22.

Jesus visited friends in Bethany, near Jerusalem. Read John 11:17-20 and Luke 10:38-42.

Jesus told a story of a man going down the road from Jerusalem to Jericho. Thieves attacked the man. Read Luke 10:25-37.

Bethlehem

Michael and his family stayed in Jerusalem for over a week, celebrating the Passover. Then, they made a short trip to Bethlehem. Bethlehem is a small town five miles south of Jerusalem.

"This is the City of David," Michael's father said. "But it was here before the time of David. It was called Ephrath in early times, and Rachel is buried near here."

Michael looked up from the road at the town above. Bethlehem was built on a ridge. The road that went from Jerusalem to Hebron, and on to Egypt, ran below the town.

"What's that up there?" Michael asked, pointing to a cone-shaped hill on beyond Bethlehem. The hill had a magnificent fortress at its top.

Michael's father spoke in anger. "That's Herod's palace! And his tomb too! Evil man that he was! And his sons no less evil!"

"We came only to see our family," said Michael's mother, gently. "Look, there they are."

Michael enjoyed his visit at Bethlehem. He ran through its narrow streets with his cousin. He played in a field nearby, where shepherds tended their sheep.

Late one evening as Michael and his cousin returned from playing, they saw women at a well.

"That well has been here forever," said Michael's cousin.

Michael laughed. "Forever?"

"Well, for a long, long time. My father says King David's soldiers broke through the Philistine army lines to get water from the well. They brought the water back to David, because he had wished for some." (The story is found in I Chronicles 11:17-19.)

"You're right," said Michael, in awe. "That is an old, old well. You must like living in David's city."

In Old Testament times, Naomi, Ruth, and Boaz lived in Bethlehem. Naomi had lived there before she went to Moab. Naomi returned with Ruth.

King David was born in Bethlehem and grew up there. At that time, Bethlehem was a walled city. Samuel came to Bethlehem to anoint David as king of Israel.

Jesus in Bethlehem

Jesus was born in Bethlehem. Micah had said He would be born there. Read Micah 5:2.

Mary and Joseph went to Bethlehem to register to be taxed. While they were there, Jesus was born. Read Luke 2:1-7.

Shepherds came to worship Jesus. Read Luke 2:8-16.

Later, Wise-men came. Read Matthew 2:1-12.

Sea of Salt

The Dead Sea, or Salt Sea, is east of Bethlehem. It is 46 miles long and about 10 miles across.

This body of water is the lowest in the world. The Jordan River and some little streams flow into the Dead Sea. But no water flows out. The only water that leaves the Dead Sea is the water that evaporates. Since the climate is hot and dry, much water evaporates, leaving behind minerals that were in the water.

This helps explain why the Dead Sea is so salty—four times as salty as ocean water.

Nothing can grow in the Dead Sea—no plants, no fish, not even the algae that so often grows in stagnant water. This is because there is so much magnesium bromide in the water. The magnesium bromide is poisonous.

There is a salt-deposit mountain on the southeast shore of the Dead Sea. It is called Mount Sodom, and people have collected salt from it for centuries.

WILDERNESS. Between Bethlehem and the Dead Sea, there is a wilderness area called the Wilderness of Judea. This land has always been barren, desolate.

DEAD SEA SCROLLS. About 40 years ago, some ancient scrolls were found in a cave near the Dead Sea. Some were copies of Scriptures, about 2,000 years old.

THE DEAD SEA SECT. In New Testament times, a group of people settled at Qumran, near the Dead Sea. These people lived a simple life and shared their belongings. They may have been the people who hid the Dead Sea scrolls in the caves. More scrolls were found in their settlement. Scholars think these people may have been Essenes.

MASADA is a natural-rock fortress. After Jesus' death, when the Romans fought the Jews, 960 Jews fled to Masada. But the Romans conquered Masada in 73 A.D.

MACHERUS was a fort and palace belonging to King Herod Antipas. It was on the east side of the Dead Sea. Herod arrested John the Baptist, because John had condemned Herod for stealing his brother's wife. Herod held John a prisoner at Macherus. Finally, Herod had John killed at this fortress.

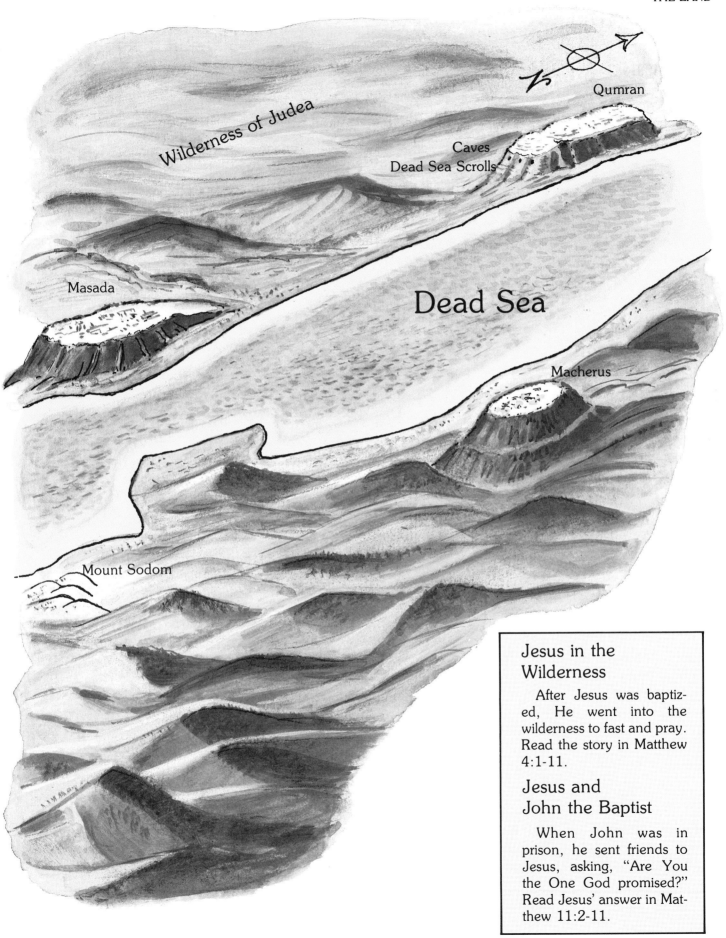

Wilderness of Judea

Qumran

Caves
Dead Sea Scrolls

Masada

Dead Sea

Macherus

Mount Sodom

Jesus in the Wilderness

After Jesus was baptized, He went into the wilderness to fast and pray. Read the story in Matthew 4:1-11.

Jesus and John the Baptist

When John was in prison, he sent friends to Jesus, asking, "Are You the One God promised?" Read Jesus' answer in Matthew 11:2-11.

Along the River Jordan

Michael and his family left Bethlehem and began their journey back to their home. They retraced their steps until they reached the Jordan River.

Michael may not have known it, but the Jordan River was—and is—a fairly small river. At its north end, four underground springs flow into four small streams. Their names are Nahr Banias, Ain Leddan, Nahr Hasbani, and Nahr Bareighit.

The Nahr Banias begins in a cave near the town of Caesarea Philippi.

The Ain Leddan (or Spring of Dan) begins near the city of Dan, mentioned in the Old Testament.

The Nahr Hasbani is the longest stream. It travels 24 miles before becoming the Jordan.

The Nahr Bareighit has several beautiful waterfalls. It seems strange that its name means "the flea river." However, it is a very small mountain stream.

In New Testament times, the Jordan River widened into a small lake, called Lake Hula, then narrowed to a river again. Today, that area is mostly farmland.

Ten miles south of this ancient lake, the river Jordan widens into the Sea of Galilee.

From the Sea of Galilee, the Jordan flows south again toward the Dead Sea. The Jordan Valley is about 70 miles long. However, the river twists and turns so much that its water travels about 200 miles. There are rapids and small waterfalls along the way.

Many more streams join the Jordan before it reaches the Dead Sea. The Yarmuk is the largest.

Finally, the Jordan enters the Dead Sea.

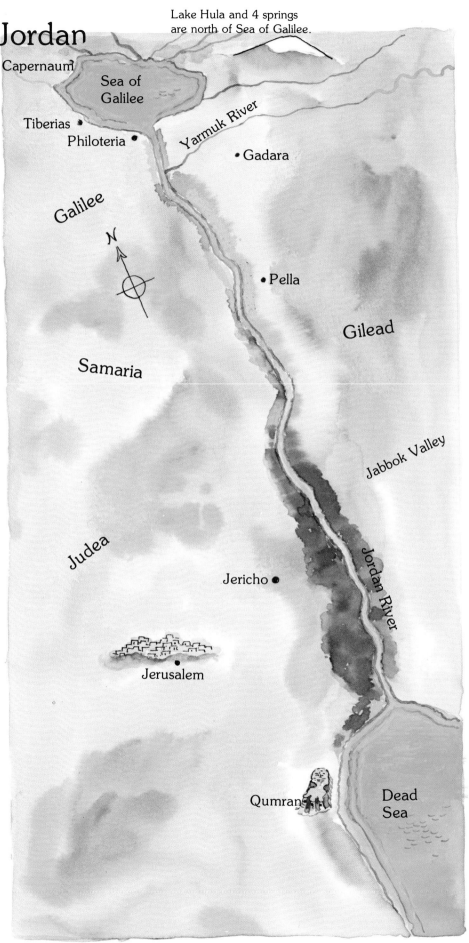

Lake Hula and 4 springs are north of Sea of Galilee.

Capernaum

Sea of Galilee

Tiberias

Philoteria

Yarmuk River

Gadara

Galilee

Pella

Gilead

Samaria

Jabbok Valley

Judea

Jericho

Jordan River

Jerusalem

Qumran

Dead Sea

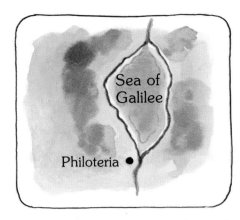

HOT SPRINGS. Not far from the Jordan River were the towns of Gadara and Pella. In both of these towns, there were natural hot springs. In New Testament times, Greek and Roman people liked to come to bathe in these hot springs. The hot mineral water was very soothing. Some people thought it helped cure illness.

PHILOTERIA was a town located where the Jordan formed again from the Sea of Galilee. Travelers often crossed the Jordan at Philoteria, to go around Samaria.

GILEAD. The land east of the Jordan, between the Yarmuk and Jabbok Rivers and all along the Jabbok valley, was called Gilead. This area had beautiful, fertile land. Some of the early tribes of Israel decided to stay there instead of crossing over Jordan into the promised land with the rest of the tribes. The story can be found in Numbers, chapter 32.

BETHABARA was a place along the Jordan where John the Baptist preached and baptized people. No one knows for sure where this town was located.

Ruins of Jericho

JERICHO is one of the oldest cities in the world. It was the most important city near the Jordan when Joshua arrived there. Joshua and the Israelites captured and destroyed it when they entered the promised land. The city was rebuilt when Ahab was king. In New Testament times, Jericho was an important city. Groves of palm trees grew there.

Jesus Near the Jordan River

Jesus came to the Jordan to be baptized by John the Baptist. Read Matthew 3:13-17.

Jesus traveled along the Jordan River on some of His trips.

Jesus spent time in Jericho. He met Zacchaeus there. Read Luke 19:2-10.

Samaria

Samaria was the land between Judea and Galilee. People aren't sure just where Judea ended and Samaria began, but it was somewhere north of Jerusalem, perhaps near Bethel. The Romans didn't think of Samaria as a separate country at all. To them, both Judea and Samaria were ruled by Pontius Pilate.

To Michael and his family, though, Samaria was a separate country. The Jews and Samaritans were enemies. So Michael and his family went around Samaria on their trips to and from Jerusalem.

Samaria had been an important part of the promised land. Joseph's bones were brought to Shechem and buried there.

But by New Testament times, the Jews and Samaritans were separate races. Most of the Israelites in Samaria had been taken away as captives by the Assyrians. The Assyrians brought in Assyrians to live in Samaria.

These new people intermarried with the Israelites who were left in Samaria. Their religion became a mixture of the Assyrian religions and the Jewish religion.

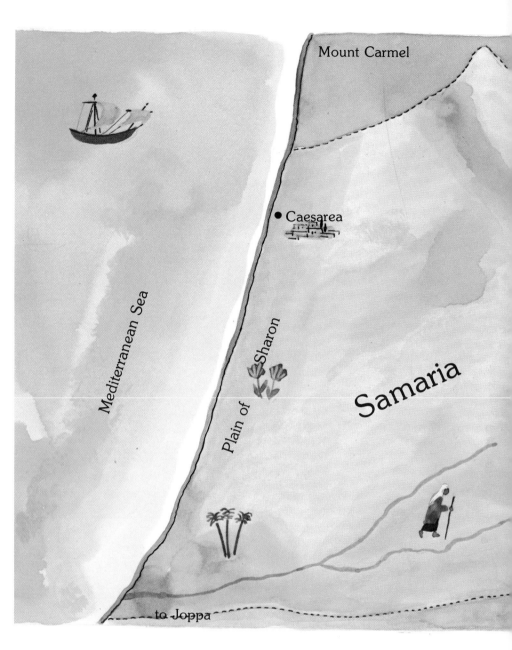

THE CITY OF SAMARIA. This city lies near the center of Samaria. The sixth king of Israel, Omri, made Samaria his capital. Later, Herod the Great had a home in this city.

PLAIN OF SHARON. Along the coast of the Mediterranean Sea, between Joppa and Mount Carmel, there is a plain, or flat land area, called the Plain of Sharon. In New Testament times, many Gentiles lived here. It had rich farmland and beautiful oak forests. Herod the Great built a seaport, Caesarea, on its coastline.

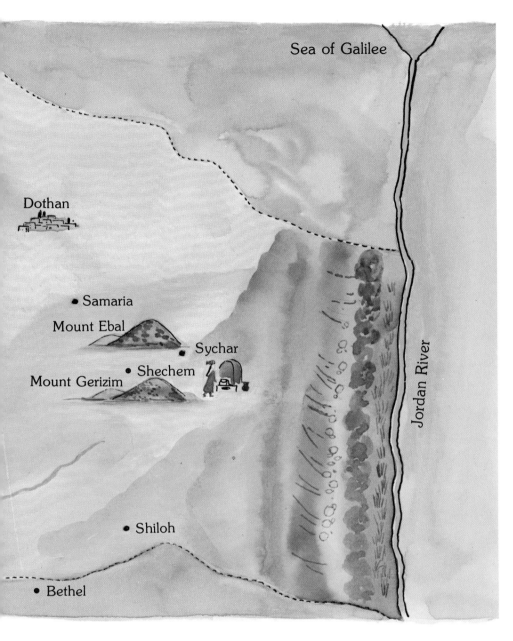

Sea of Galilee

Dothan

Samaria

Mount Ebal

Sychar

Mount Gerizim

Shechem

Jordan River

Shiloh

Bethel

The tabernacle

Important cities and towns in Samaria included Shechem, Shiloh, and Apollonia. The tabernacle was kept at Shiloh until the time of Samuel.

Two important mountains in Samaria were Mount Gerizim and Mount Ebal. They are close together. Gerizim is 2,849 feet high. Ebal is 3,077 feet high.

JACOB'S WELL. At Sychar, there was a well called Jacob's well. Jesus talked to a Samaritan woman there. The two discussed the differences between Jewish and Samaritan religions. Sychar and the well were near the land that Jacob gave to his son Joseph. This means they were near Shechem, on the eastern side of Mount Ebal.

Jesus in Samaria

Jesus did travel through Samaria. Unlike most Jews, Jesus treated Samaritans with kindness. He spoke to the woman at Jacob's well. Read John, chapter 4.

On one occasion, Jesus healed ten lepers. One was a Samaritan. Read Luke 17:11-19.

And Jesus told a story about a Samaritan. Read Luke 10:25-37.

Galilee

North of Samaria lay the region of Galilee. Michael knew about cities and towns in the eastern part of Galilee. He had traveled through Magdala and Tiberias and Philoteria many times. He and his family would come back through these towns on this trip too.

And, of course, Michael knew about his own home town, Capernaum. He also knew about the surrounding area.

He did not know cities and towns to the west as well. They included Cana, Nazareth, and Nain, which are mentioned in the Bible.

Galilee is not a very large province. It is about 30 miles from its west edge to its east edge. From north to south is about 50 miles. Travelers in Bible times would take several days to travel 50 miles.

Galilee is the highest and coolest part of Palestine. Winter rains bring it plenty of water. Upper Galilee has rugged mountains and oak forests. It also has plains areas where farming is good. Lower Galilee is less hilly, and the farmland is even better.

In New Testament times, the main highway going east from the Mediterranean Sea ran through Galilee. This road and an important north-south road made Galilee a thriving, prosperous place.

There was strong rivalry between Judea and Galilee. People in Judea thought Galileans were back-country people. Judeans laughed at the accent of people from Galilee.

Sculpture found at Tiberias

TIBERIAS. Herod Antipas enlarged this city and made it his capital during Jesus' lifetime. Part of it was built over a graveyard. This made it unclean, so Jews avoided the city.

CANA was in Galilee. The picture above shows Kafr Kanna as it looks today. This may be the Cana in the Bible, where Jesus performed a miracle. Or, a town named Kana-el-Jelil may have been Cana. Often, it is difficult for scholars and archaeologists to be sure about places mentioned in the New Testament.

Jesus in Galilee

Jesus grew up in Nazareth of Galilee. Read Matthew 21:11 and Mark 1:9.

Jesus' first miracle was performed at Cana. Read John 2:11. While Jesus was in Cana, He healed a boy. Read John 4:46-53.

At Nain, Jesus raised a widow's son from the dead. Read Luke 7:11-15.

MOUNT TABOR. This mountain is in southern Galilee. It is 1,843 feet high. It looks like an upside-down bowl. In the Old Testament, when Deborah was judge, an Israelite army gathered on this mountain. The general, Barak, took the army to fight against Caananites. The Israelite army won the battle. Barak and Deborah sang a song of praise to God for the victory.

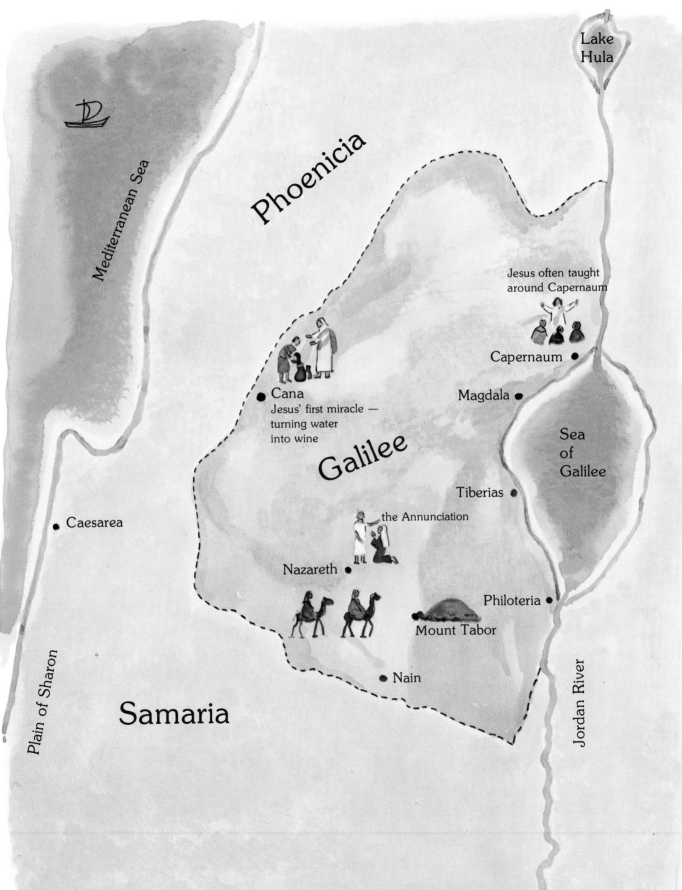

Lake
Hula

Phoenicia

Mediterranean Sea

Jesus often taught
around Capernaum

Capernaum

Cana

Jesus' first miracle —
turning water
into wine

Magdala

Sea
of
Galilee

Galilee

Tiberias

Caesarea

the Annunciation

Nazareth

Philoteria

Mount Tabor

Nain

Plain of Sharon

Samaria

Jordan River

Nazareth

"This isn't the road home," Michael said as he and his family turned westward from the Sea of Galilee.

"No," said his father. "We will stop in Nazareth before going home. My uncle lives in Nazareth." So all that day and into the next, Michael and his family walked.

Finally . . . "There! See? There is Nazareth." From the hilltop, Michael could see the town.

Michael and his family entered Nazareth. Through busy, crowded streets they walked. The streets were narrow, with houses close by on both sides. Michael saw a carpenter's shop.

"Here is the house," Michael's father said at last.

What a welcome awaited them! Michael's great uncle was so glad to see them! Soon all their feet had been washed, and a lovely meal was set before them.

"Nazareth may not be as large as your city of Capernaum," said the uncle, "but we do know how to welcome our guests."

"Yes," said Michael's father. "We feel very welcome."

Jesus in Nazareth

Mary and Joseph were from Nazareth. They left there before Jesus' birth to go to Bethlehem. From Bethlehem, they went into Egypt. Read Luke 2:4; Matthew 2:13, 14.

When Mary and Joseph returned from Egypt, they brought Jesus to Nazareth. They had thought about returning to Judea instead of to Nazareth. But Herod the Great's son, Archelaus, had become ruler of Judea. Mary and Joseph feared Archelaus. Read Matthew 2:19-23.

Jesus grew up in Nazareth. After He began His ministry, He returned to Nazareth. He went to the synagogue. Leaders asked Him to read the Scriptures. Jesus read a passage from Isaiah about a preacher sent from God. "I am that preacher," Jesus said.

"You're just Joseph's son!" the people answered. They became so angry at Jesus, for claiming to be sent from God, that they tried to kill him. Read Luke 4:16-30.

In Jesus' time, people didn't think much of Nazareth. Nathanael asked, "Can any good come out of Nazareth?" But Nathanael changed his mind. Read John 1:45-49.

There is an ancient well in Nazareth. It was probably there in New Testament times. Today, it is called Mary's well, because Jesus' mother probably used it.

Nazareth had a synagogue. Michael and his family went there to worship, for they stayed over the Sabbath. Michael's father was asked to read Scripture.

Outside of Nazareth, there is a high cliff. This may have been the place where the angry people of Nazareth took Jesus, to try to kill Him. But no one knows for sure.

A Beautiful Blue Lake

Coming back from Nazareth, Michael and his family reached the Sea of Galilee.

"I feel like I'm almost home," Michael told his sister.

"Me too. Just seeing our blue sea makes me feel glad!"

As the family walked along the shores of the lake, they watched the sun glint on its waters. They saw fishing boats and fishermen casting their nets into the sea.

"This must be the prettiest place in the whole world," said Michael.

His father laughed. "Many people think that about other seas," he said. "But our harp-shaped sea is truly beautiful."

Many people in New Testament times would have agreed with Michael and his family. A Jewish rabbi said, "Jehovah hath created seven seas, but the Sea of Gennesaret is His delight."

The Sea of Gennesaret was another name for the Sea of Galilee. Still a third name was the Sea of Chinnereth. In Hebrew, the word Chinnereth means "harp-shaped."

The Sea of Galilee is about 13 miles long and 7 or 8 miles wide. In its deepest places, it is 150 feet deep. Fish abound in its waters.

Fishing was very important on the Sea of Galilee. That is how many people made their living.

Many people settled near the Sea of Galilee. Towns and cities ringed its shores.

MAGDALA. This city is on the western coast of the Sea of Galilee. Mary Magdalene was from Magdala. Today, the village is called Migdal.

GENNESARET. On the northwest shore of the Sea of Galilee, there was a plain called the Plain of Gennesaret. Good farmland was plentiful on this plain.

BETHSAIDA. This town was a small fishing village. Jesus had three disciples, Andrew, Peter, and Philip, who were from the village of Bethsaida.

Jesus and the Sea of Galilee

Jesus walked by the Sea of Galilee and called four fishermen to be His disciples. They were Simon Peter, Andrew, James, and John. Read Matthew 4:18-22.

Jesus taught from a boat just off the shore of the Sea. And He helped the fishermen find fish. Read Luke 5:1-7.

Jesus stilled a great storm on the Sea. Read Mark 4:35-41.

Near the Sea of Galilee, in the country of the Gadarenes, Jesus healed a man. Read Luke 8:26-39.

Once Jesus fed at least 5,000 people near the Sea of Galilee. Read Luke 9:10-17.

Jesus walked on the sea and helped Peter walk on it too. Read Matthew 14:22-34.

Storms rose quickly on the Sea of Galilee. They were caused by cold air sweeping in from the north and hitting warm air from the lake. The wind could be fierce.

Michael and his family reached their home safely. They'd had a long trip and seen much of their land. They were tired and glad to be home.

We'll leave Michael and his family now and travel to lands around Palestine. Much of the material in the following sections is background information. It is helpful for understanding what life was like when Jesus lived on earth.

Tyre and Sidon

Tyre and Sidon were two cities on the coast of the Mediterranean Sea. They were north of Galilee. Both were famous as seaports.

Tyre and Sidon were old, old cities. They already were important when Joshua brought the Israelites into the promised land. They were the two main cities of the Phoenician people. The Phoenicians were great sea travelers and they gave the world a simple alphabet.

Tyre and Sidon are mentioned many times in the Old Testament. King David was friendly with Hiram, the king of Tyre. Hiram sent cedar trees, and carpenters to help David build his palace.

Hiram was also a good friend to King Solomon. Hiram sent material and workers to help build Solomon's temple.

Jezebel (the wife of Ahab, king of Israel) came from Sidon, where her father was king. Jezebel tried to kill the prophets of God.

From near Tyre and Sidon came the beautiful cedars of Lebanon and a precious purple dye called "Tyrian purple."

All during New Testament times, these two cities were important trade centers. Rome conquered them and made them independent cities within the province called Syria. Each city governed much land outside the city. The region of Tyre bordered on Galilee. The region of Sidon was north of Tyre.

Jesus in Tyre and Sidon

Jesus and His disciples made a trip into the regions of Tyre and Sidon. (We don't know whether or not they actually went into the cities.) While they were there, a woman asked Jesus to heal her daughter. Read Mark 7:24-31.

Another time, people from Tyre and Sidon came to hear Jesus preach and to have Jesus heal them. Read Mark 3:7-10.

Caesarea Philippi

Caesarea Philippi was a town in Bashan, the region governed by Philip. Philip was a son of Herod the Great. The region was north of Galilee and east of Tyre and Sidon. The town was located on the slopes of snowy Mount Hermon.

A town named Paneas stood at this site earlier. It existed for centuries and centuries. But Jewish people hadn't gone there much, for at Paneas, people worshiped the god Pan.

When Philip came to power, he made Paneas his capital. He changed the name to Caesarea, in honor of the Caesar, the Roman emperor. Then, because there were already so many cities named Caesarea, he added Philippi.

Like Tyre and Sidon, Caesarea Philippi governed the region around the city.

Today, there is a village on the same site. People call the village Banias or Benaias.

Inscription honoring Philip

PHILIP. This son of Herod the Great ruled his province peacefully for 37 years. He remained loyal to Rome. Philip was more just and generous than Herod's other sons.

PAN. Pan, a Greek god, was supposed to take care of shepherds, sheep, forest animals, and hunters. Niches in rock walls near Caesarea Philippi once held statues of Pan.

Jesus and Simon Peter

Jesus and his followers once traveled to Caesarea Philippi. There, Jesus asked His disciples who He was. Read Simon Peter's answer in Matthew 16:13-18.

Near Caesarea Philippi there are high rock cliffs. These may have been visible when Jesus named Simon Peter "the rock."

Palestine's Other Neighbors

Palestine, the land in which Jesus lived, included Judea, Samaria, and Galilee. To the north of Palestine was Syria; Tyre and Sidon were in Syria. (Find these places on the map.)

Beside Syria, and east of the Sea of Galilee, was Bashan, where Philip reigned. Caesarea Philippi was in Bashan.

South of Bashan was the Decapolis, then Perea, then Nabatea.

Many Jewish people lived in these surrounding areas. Here is some information about these neighbors of Palestine.

SYRIA. Syria was north of Galilee. Tyre and Sidon were in the province of Syria. Actually, so was Palestine, in the eyes of the Romans. The Romans had made Palestine part of the province of Syria in 64 B.C.

The Jews, though, thought of themselves as separate from Syria.

Today, the country of Lebanon is in this area.

BASHAN. Philip, the son of Herod the Great, ruled in this section. His father had ruled there earlier.

Today, this region is part of the country of Syria.

DECAPOLIS. Decapolis means "ten cities." And ten cities joined together in a league to make up this territory. (Later, more cities joined the league; but it kept its name.) Most of the cities were on the east side of the Jordan River. But one, Scythopolis, was on the west side, between Galilee and Samaria. Scythopolis was very important to the league, for it was on an east-west trade route.

Today, this region is part of the country of Jordan.

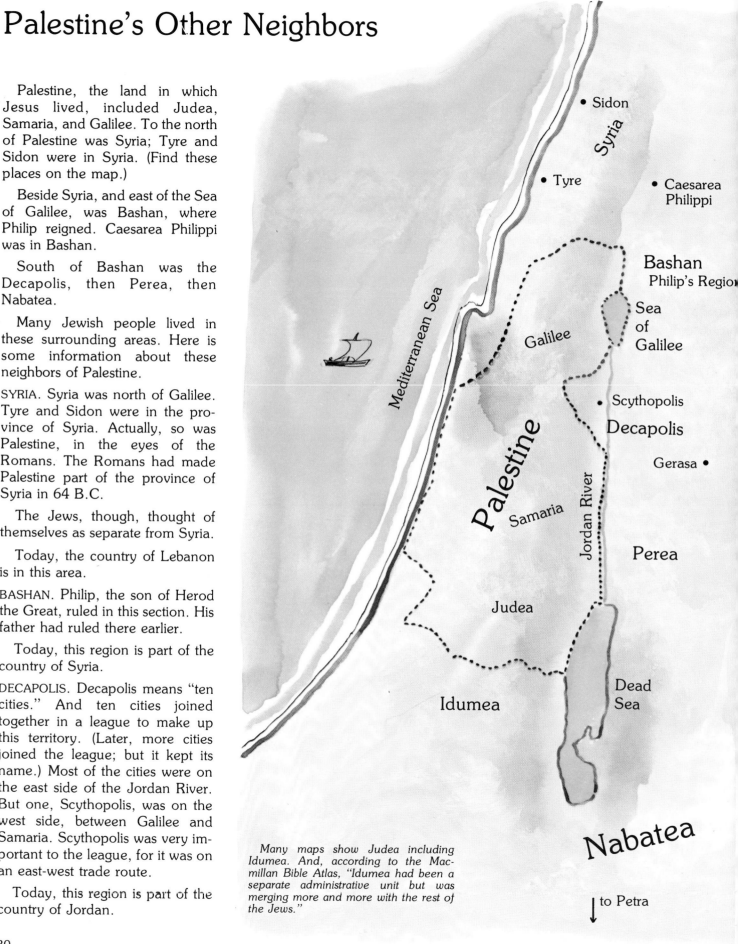

Many maps show Judea including Idumea. And, according to the Macmillan Bible Atlas, "Idumea had been a separate administrative unit but was merging more and more with the rest of the Jews."

80

Arabia

PEREA. East of the Jordan River was Perea, "the land beyond." Herod Antipas ruled in Perea. Today, this region is part of the country of Jordan.

NABATEA. Farther south was Nabatea. The Nabateans were an Arabian people. They were nomads and traders. Israel and Jordan are in this area today.

IDUMEA. Idumea was west of the Dead Sea. In Old Testament times, it was called Edom. Esau, Jacob's brother, went to live in this area.

Today, this land is in the country of Israel.

PETRA was the capital city of the Nabateans. The Nabateans carved magnificient temples out of the rose-red sandstone cliffs of this city. These temples still can be seen.

At Gerasa, in the Decapolis, there was a forum. In Roman and Greek cities, a forum was like a town square. It was the central place of business. Here people gathered for meetings and to buy and sell merchandise. Public trials often were held in a forum. Archeologists have found the ruins of this forum at Gerasa.

Jesus in Perea and the Decapolis

Jesus was baptized near Bethabara, which was "beyond Jordan." Bethabara probably was in Perea. Read John 1:28.

Jesus' kinsman, John the Baptist, was killed at Macherus, in Perea.

Gadara was one of the "ten cities." Near Gadara, Jesus freed a man of demons. In the Decapolis, Jesus was popular. Read Matthew 4:24, 25.

Jesus fed a crowd of more than 4,000 while he was in the Decapolis region. Read Matthew 15:32-38.

Jesus traveled through Perea and the Decapolis on his way to and from Jerusalem. And he taught in Perea. Read the account in John 10:40-42.

While Jesus was in Perea, He blessed the children. Read Luke 18:15-17.

The Greeks

Greece is a small peninsula across the Mediterranean Sea from Palestine. (A peninsula is a part of the land that sticks out into a lake or ocean.) Jewish people didn't know much about Greece until after they returned from Babylon. (This return was over 400 years before the time of Christ.) But even as the Jews were rebuilding Jerusalem, the Greeks were becoming powerful.

In 334 B.C., Alexander the Great, of Greece, decided to conquer Persia. He conquered many other nations as well. The Jewish people were among those he conquered.

Greek leaders ruled Palestine until 167 B.C. During these 165 years, Greek ways of life and Greek thinking became important in Jewish life.

Here are a few important things to know about the Greeks.

1. The Greeks thought a lot about life—what the universe was like, how people should live, how people should think. They made this kind of thinking into an art and a careful discipline. They even gave it a name—philosophy.

2. The Greeks were among the first to carefully study science and medicine.

3. Greek art, music, drama, and literature were all of very high quality. Today, people still read Greek stories and poetry.

4. Greeks made their language important in all the countries they captured. People everywhere spoke Greek. The New Testament was written in the Greek language.

5. The architecture of Greece spread throughout the world.

6. The Greeks loved freedom. Their ideas about freedom are still important.

OLYMPICS. Greeks thought exercise was very important. Every four years, the Greeks held athletic contests. The modern Olympics are based on this Greek idea.

THE PARTHENON. The Greeks built a temple to the goddess Athene. Its ruins still can be seen in Athens. The Parthenon shows what Greek architecture was like.

Greek Rulers in Palestine

Alexander the Great ruled from 332 B.C. until he died in 323 B.C.

In 301 B.C., Ptolemy, one of Alexander's generals, took over Palestine. Ptolemy and his heirs ruled Palestine until 198 B.C.

Another of Alexander's generals was Seleucus. He and his heirs ruled Syria. (In fact, they often were called Syrians, even though they were originally Greeks.) Then the Seleucids took over Palestine too. The last Seleucid to rule in Palestine was Antiochus IV.

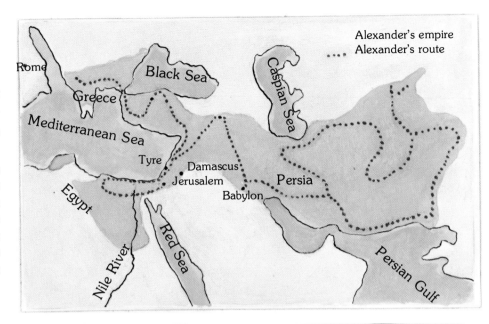

DRAMA. Greek people loved plays. They built beautiful outdoor theaters everywhere they moved. The pictured ruins are what is left of the Greek theater in Athens.

ALEXANDER THE GREAT was a military genius. He formed his foot soldiers in phalanxes. This means he lined them up in rows, standing so close together that their shields touched. Their long spears had to be fitted in between the soldiers in front of them. This mosaic was found at Pompeii. It shows Alexander the Great on his horse.

GREEK CITIES. In Palestine, as in other places, Greeks built their own cities, using their kinds of architecture. Greek people flocked to these cities.

The Septuagint

Many Jewish people lived in places other than Palestine. And many Jews spoke Greek. So, in Egypt, a Greek translation of the Old Testament was made. This happened between 280 and 180 B.C. The translation was called Septuagint.

Septuagint means "70." It is said that 72 scholars, six from each of the tribes of Israel, made the translation.

This translation is still very important to Biblical scholars.

The Romans

As Greek rulers began to lose power, Roman rulers gained power. Rome is on another peninsula across the Mediterranean from Palestine. The Romans were excellent warriors. Roman rulers were determined to conquer all the land across the Mediterranean Sea.

As the Romans took over regions, they built fortresses and cities and public buildings. And they built roads.

By the end of the Roman rule, there were roads in every part of the Roman Empire. These roads lasted for centuries. Some still exist.

In 63 B.C., Pompey, a Roman ruler, marched on Jerusalem. He captured the temple.

Roman generals appointed Herod the Great as Palestine's king. He reigned from 37 B.C. until 4 B.C.

The Jews revolted against Rome in 67 A.D. Rome sent a general, Titus, to recapture the area. In 70 A.D., Titus captured Jerusalem. He burned down the temple and left Jerusalem in ruins.

The Romans ruled in Palestine until 638 A.D.

Jesus and Rome

Mary and Joseph went to Bethlehem because a Roman emperor made a decree. Read Luke 2:1-7.

Jesus did not preach rebellion against Rome. He even healed the servant of a Roman soldier. Read Matthew 8:5-13.

A Roman governor, Pontius Pilate, condemned Jesus to die. Read Matthew 27:11-26.

ROMAN BUILDERS. The Romans were great builders. They built aquaducts to bring water into the cities. The picture above shows the ruins of the aquaduct they built in Caesarea. Romans also built strong, durable roads. And they built theaters and stadiums, temples and monuments, walls, fortresses, high towers and palaces.

The Egyptians

ROMAN OPPRESSORS. The Romans were tough-minded conquerors. They killed many people, took many more as slaves, and taxed everyone. Most Jews hated them.

ROMAN GODS. Romans worshiped many gods. They even made their rulers gods. They gladly added other people's gods. They didn't like the Jewish idea of one God.

EGYPT was close to Palestine. So from the time of Abraham on, the histories of the Egyptians and the Jewish people were intertwined. Sometimes Jews and Egyptians were enemies; sometimes they were friends. Egypt had been a great power at a point in Old Testament times. But, by New Testament times, Egypt was no longer a major power.

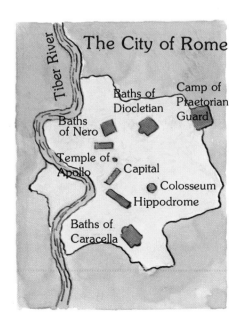

ALEXANDRIA. In Egypt, as in Palestine, the Greeks built their own cities. One of these was Alexandria. Many Jews lived there. A library and university were there.

Jesus in Egypt

When Herod the Great wanted to kill the baby Jesus, Mary and Joseph fled to Egypt. They lived there until Herod died. Read Matthew 2:13-23.

Between the Old and New Testaments

The Maccabeans

Greek rulers let the Jews worship as they wished until Antiochus IV became their ruler in 175 B.C. Antiochus said that all his people must worship the Greek god, Zeus.

Antiochus sent troops to Jerusalem in 168 B.C. They seized the temple and offered sacrifices of pigs on the altar. Jews thought pigs were unclean animals. So the act of sacrificing pigs was a terrible insult to all Jewish people. Jews were ordered to worship Zeus. Many died because they refused.

In the town of Modin, Antiochus' officers found a priest named Mattathias. They ordered him to offer a sacrifice to Zeus. Mattathias was an old man. He refused. "I and my sons will walk in the covenant of our fathers," he said.

The king's officers found another priest, who would obey them. So Mattathias killed this priest and a king's officer too. Then he and his sons fled to the mountains between Jericho and Jerusalem. They began a war against the Greeks.

When Mattathias died, his third son, Judas Maccabeus, took over. Judas recaptured the temple from the Greeks on the 25th day of Kislev, in 165 B.C. To this day, Jewish people celebrate Chanukah, or Hanukkah, in memory of that victory.

Judas died in battle, and Jonathan, the youngest son of Mattathias, took over.

Jonathan became ruler and also high priest. He fought on until he was put to death. Simon, another son, took charge.

In 143 B.C., Simon took all of Jerusalem from the Greeks. In 141 B.C., the Greeks granted independence to Simon and his followers. The Maccabeans had won.

The Hasmoneans, Descendants of Maccabeans

Simon, the last son of Mattathias, was killed in 135 B.C.

Monument of John Hyrcanus

Simon was the first ruler in the Hasmonean dynasty. Simon's son, John Hyrcanus, became king upon Simon's death.

The Hasmoneans ruled until 63 B.C., when the Romans conquered Jerusalem. Even then, the Romans left a Hasmonean in power, as their governor. He was John Hyrcanus, the Second.

While John Hyrcanus was governor of Palestine, Herod was governor of Galilee. Herod later became King Herod.

CHANUKAH. The feast of Chanukah or Hanukkah is also called the feast of Lights. The celebration lasts eight days. People light candles and sing hymns.

MACCABEAN TOMBS. At the town of Modin, half way between Joppa and Jerusalem, there are rock-cut tombs. Tradition says these are the tombs of the Maccabees.

COIN. This coin was made in the time of Antiochus IV. On the front of the coin, there is a picture of Antiochus IV. On the back, there is a picture of his favorite god, Zeus.

From Chasidim to Pharisee

When the Jews were captives in Babylon, a group of people kept alive the Jewish faith. These people called themselves the Chasidim, the "pious."

When the Jews returned to Jerusalem, these Chasidim made sure everything was done just right. The temple had to be built like Solomon's temple. The ways of worship had to be restored to what they had been before the exile.

The Chasidim hated the Greeks.

When the Maccabean revolt came, most of the Chasidim joined it. In time, the Chasidim became the Pharisees.

Pharisee means "separate one." More and more, the Pharisees set themselves apart. First they separated themselves from the Greeks. Then they separated themselves from all who sympathized with the Greeks. Finally, the Pharisees separated themselves from all who disagreed with them. They felt that, not only should Mosaic laws be followed, but also traditions of the Jewish fathers.

These were the Pharisees Jesus condemned, because they laid heavy burdens on the people.

From Friend of Greeks to Sadducee

As Greek rule continued in Palestine, some priests took on Greek ideas. Some wore Greek hats and liked Greek games.

These priests even took a team of athletes to compete in Greek games at Tyre. They walked in a parade in honor of a foreign god. Jewish people were outraged.

These priests managed to get one of their group appointed as high priest. He convinced Antiochus IV that Jewish people were ready to adopt Greek values. That was when Antiochus IV sent in his troops.

These priests took no part in the Maccabean revolt. But priesthood was passed on from father to son. So even after the Maccabeans won, these priests were important. This group, and others who agreed with them, became the Sadducees.

Under Roman rule, Sadducees were "friends of Romans" as they had been "friends of Greeks."

Even in Jesus' time, there seemed to be only one thing Sadducees and Pharisees agreed upon: that Jesus was dangerous and should be killed.

Who Was Who in Palestine

Herod the Great

Herod the Great began his career as a governor of Galilee under John Hyrcanus, the Second. Soon the Parthians invaded Palestine from the north, killing John Hyrcanus and Herod's brother Phasael. Herod escaped.

Herod battled the Parthians at Bethlehem to get to Egypt. In Egypt, he outwitted Queen Cleopatra. Then he sailed the Mediterranean Sea during winter, and finally arrived in Rome.

In Rome, Herod pleaded his case against the Parthians and won Roman support. With their backing, he returned as ruler of Palestine. Of course, he still had to conquer the country. Herod turned out to be a shrewd and ruthless warrior. Soon he was king of the Jews. The year was 37 B.C.

Through his entire reign, Herod served Rome. He built Caesarea on the Mediterranean coast.

Among the Jews, Herod built up a political party called the Herodians. These were Jews who courted Herod's favor.

Herod built other cities, restored fortresses, built roads and palaces. Then he began his great project—rebuilding the temple.

Herod was known to many as a cruel ruler. He thought nothing of killing those who opposed him. He even killed his wife and two sons.

As Herod grew older, he seems to have become insane. Probably his madness was due to hardening of the arteries in his brain. He became more and more violent. He thought everybody was against him. He ordered the killing of the babies in Bethlehem shortly before he died in 4 B.C.

In his will, Herod divided his kingdom among his three sons.

Herod Antipas

Coin minted by Herod Antipas

When Herod the Great died, his son Herod Antipas became ruler of Galilee and Perea. Herod Antipas remained loyal to Rome. He was also as ruthless as his father.

Herod Antipas decided he wanted the title of king in 36 A.D. He asked the Roman emperor, Tiberius, to give him that title. However, Herod's nephew told Tiberius that Herod was planning treason. The story was a lie, but Tiberius believed it. In 40 A.D., he sent Herod into exile.

Two More Sons of Herod

Coin minted by Archelaus

Inscription on pedestal honoring Philip

ARCHELAUS became ruler of Judea. But he ruled so stupidly and cruelly that Rome sent him into exile in 6 A.D. Then Rome sent a governor to rule Judea.

PHILIP. The third son to gain a province was Philip. Philip received Bashan. Philip's reign was more peaceful than that of his brothers.

Two Caesars

AUGUSTUS CAESAR. "Caesar" was the title for the Roman emperor. Augustus Caesar ruled the Roman empire from 31 B.C. until 14 A.D.

TIBERIUS CAESAR. This emperor ruled from 14 A.D. to 37 A.D. Tiberius had a morbid fear of disloyalty. He tried many people for treason.

Jesus, John the Baptist, and the Two Herods

Herod the Great was king when Jesus was born. The Wise-men went to Herod for information. Read Matthew 2:1-16.

Herod Antipas ruled when Jesus and John the Baptist were adults. This Herod had John killed. Read Matthew 14:3-12.

Herod Antipas mocked Jesus at Jesus' trial. Read Luke 23:6-12.

Pontius Pilate

Inscription to Pilate

Pilate was a Roman governor in charge of Judea. He ruled from 26 to 36 A.D. Often governors didn't do much more than collect taxes. But Palestine was such a difficult place to rule, that the governor had supreme authority. He answered only to the emperor.

Pilate seemed to enjoy offending the Jews. In the temple, he hung up golden shields with pictures of Roman gods on them. He took some of the temple money to build an aquaduct.

Usually, Pilate lived in Caesarea, but at feast times, when pilgrims filled Jerusalem, Pilate came to Jerusalem.

Pilate condemned Jesus to death for political reasons. The Jews insisted and threatened to complain to Tiberius that Pilate had sided with a traitor.

Pilate was sent back to Rome in 36 A.D. because his troops killed innocent people in Samaria. It is said that he killed himself soon after that.

Flavius Josephus

People today know a lot about Palestine during the time of Jesus. Some information comes from the Gospels. But the writers of Matthew, Mark,

Luke and John were interested mostly in Jesus. They didn't pay a lot of attention to other matters.

A historian named Flavius Josephus recorded much information about that time. Josephus was a Jew. When the Jews revolted in 63 A.D., Josephus fought with them. Soon, Josephus was captured by the Romans. He acted as an interpreter for them. Later, in Rome, he wrote official history.

Roman Rulers in the Bible

Luke said that Caesar Augustus was emperor and Quirinuis was governor of Syria when Jesus was born. Read Luke 2:1, 2.

Luke dated the time when John the Baptist began preaching by listing people, including rulers. Read Luke 3:1-3.

Pontius Pilate's role in Jesus' death is told in all four Gospels.

Jesus

Jesus was born in a tiny town, of parents who were not rich or famous or well-educated. He lived in a province that was ruled by Rome. Jesus only lived on earth 33 years. Then he was killed on the cross as a traitor.

Jesus did not know the important people of His time. He was hated by many of the leaders in Palestine. Yet, Jesus' life has changed the lives of millions.

After Jesus' resurrection and ascension, Christianity spread through the then-known world within 300 years. At first, Rome persecuted the church, but a Roman emperor, Constantine, became a Christian in the fourth century A.D.

Millions and millions of people—through almost 2,000 years—have become Christians, followers of Jesus.

Jesus offers salvation and a personal relationship with God. He set up a higher standard of what goodness is than there had been before. Jesus showed and taught love. He taught people to treat each other with kindness and justice.

No one claims that Christians have always followed Jesus' example. Yet the influence of Christians is obvious in the world. And the faith of Christians is a great help to them, and to others, in daily life. It also offers hope for life after death.

On the next page are some things the Bible tells of Jesus' life on earth.

Jesus Taught . . .

"I am the way and the truth and the life. No one comes to the Father except through me" (John 14:6).

"Let the little children come to me, and do not hinder them, for the kingdom of heaven belongs to such as these" (Matthew 19:14).

"Come to me, all you who are weary and burdened, and I will give you rest" (Matthew 11:28).

"A new commandment I give you: Love one another. As I have loved you, so you must love one another. All men will know that you are my disciples if you love one another" (John 13:34, 35).

"Love your enemies, do good to those who hate you. . . . Do to others as you would have them do to you" (Luke 6:27, 31).

"Unless a man is born again, he cannot see the kingdom of God" (John 3:3).

These verses are from the NIV.

Jesus was born in Bethlehem, of Judea. God was His Father. Angels announced His birth to shepherds, who worshiped Him. Wise-men brought Him gifts.

When Jesus was 12 years old, Mary and Joseph took Him to the temple. There Jesus astonished teachers and priests with His knowledge and wisdom.

When Jesus was 30, He was baptized in the Jordan River by John the Baptist. A voice from Heaven said, "This is my beloved Son. I am pleased with Him."

Often, great crowds of people followed Jesus. He spent time teaching them. "Blessed are the gentle," Jesus said, "and the poor and the hungry and the righteous."

Jesus healed the sick, the blind, and the crippled. He healed lepers and those who could not speak or hear. He even raised people from the dead.

Once Jesus went up on a high mountain. There He talked to Elijah and Moses. Jesus' clothing became white and shining. The three spoke of Jesus' death.

Jesus and His disciples ate a last meal together. "Eat this bread and drink this cup," Jesus said, "to remember me." Christians still remember Jesus.

Judas betrayed Jesus. The Sanhedrin condemned Jesus to die. Pilate sentenced Him. Roman soldiers nailed Him to a cross. There, He died.

On the third day after His death, Jesus rose from the dead. His disciples saw Him. So did many other people. Then Jesus returned to Heaven to be with God.

Index